IN OUR OWN WORDS

AN ANTHOLOGY

OF
POETRY

FROM A GENERATION
FALSELY LABELED

GENERATION X

edited by Marlow Peerse Weaver

mwe

In Our Own Words
Generation X Poetry

"mwe" is an imprint of MW Enterprises

Printing by Jostens
Cover artwork by Anne M. Miller

MW Enterprises
3903 Capital Blvd., Suite 194
Raleigh, NC 27604 USA

mwe@interpath.com

PRINTING HISTORY
First printing 1999

ISBN 0-9654136-2-4

Printed in the United States of America

Forward

Guess what? There is no such thing as a Generation X. The term is no more than a convenient catch-all creation of the media. Did anyone poll the age group in question and ask them to choose a label they'd be comfortable with? Certainly, "Gen X", "Slackers", or "Lost Youth" wouldn't be their choice. Our commercial, media-driven world, however, needs its sensationalized stereotypes. So we have the term "Generation X".

The designation "X" is itself something of an irony. Especially if one interprets "X" to mean the lack of any particular definition; a faceless, positionless, standing-for-nothing generation. As one poet in this book points out, perhaps that is no more than wishful thinking by preceding generations, a hostility towards youth arising out of a simmering guilt regarding their own abandonment of more idealistic values? And if that "X" is supposed to portray a generation lacking any feelings or emotions; wrong, wrong, wrong. The poetry in this book speaks for itself.

Poetry? No other living generation posts more poetry on the Internet than that generation framed by the birth years 1961- 1982. It is a generation with a huge appetite for expressing itself. And the majority of the poetry they produce isn't about disappearing into some ill-defined nirvana, or nothingness. It is a generation filled with passions, longings, joys, angst...and the will and courage to let those emotions transform themselves into words.

Before even contemplating this anthology, I placed myself in the shoes of a generation being called the Xer's. Doing so elicited a sense of a frighteningly confining box closing in around me. It was as if the world wanted to write off my inherent right to individuality, my right to free expression, my right to establish my own identity. Wouldn't I protest too, feel resentment, if the world around me dismissed my generation with the mere cross-stroking of two lines, an "X"? It troubled me too, deeply, to speculate how such labeling might affect a sense of self-worth? This process is what built up a burning within me to challenge this generation, challenge them to stand up, speak out, prove to the world they are vastly more than numbing labels like "slackers", "Lost Youth".

In issuing this challenge, why did I choose poetry as the vehicle of self-expression? First of all, it is a generation very much into poetry, witnessed by countless such sites on the Internet. In a practical sense, poetry is more concise than prose. I wanted to include as many voices as possible in a chorus of generational expression. Finally, while prose can drift off into the logical, rational, yes, sterile, poetry tends more to come from the heart and soul, and guts of those who write it.

The challenge I issued was answered loudly. Over a period of several months, thousands of poems rolled in, not clones of each other but covering the vast spectrum of the human condition. A generation proved what I had only speculated, that they are as individualistic, yes, eclectic, as any generation!

In this anthology I have attempted to honor that eclecticism. You will find poetry covering widely-varying themes, emotions, and modes of expression. But not by design, or careful editing on my part. What you read is a reflection of submissions I received, also in proportionality. If a certain percentage of the poems in this anthology relate to love, or death, it is because that proportion, of the poems submitted, addressed those themes. As editor, I merely held up a mirror to reflect how a generation chose to identity itself.

Poetry purists may wince now and then in reading through this anthology. The mission of this book, however, was never restricted to showcasing wordsmiths and their refined mechanical manipulation of words and imagery. In fact, any poetry conveying a sense of contrivance was placed in the reject bin. Sought were expressions from the hearts and souls of the writers, the hearts and souls of a generation. And as songs span a great spectrum, from operatic arias to basic folk music, poetry speaks out from and touches many divergent places in the human existence. The poems in this anthology range from sophisticated to salt of the earth, from urban and inner city to out in the hinterlands. Just as the generation that wrote it embodies more diversity than any labels or stereotypes could ever try to encompass.

You will enjoy this anthology, if you view it as an opportunity to gain insight, insight into a generation. You will enjoy this anthology, if you are of that generation and cherish an opportunity to celebrate your generation speaking out, unfettered, unfiltered, uncensored, without your elders trying to squeeze you into neat little boxes. You will enjoy this anthology, if you view it as a bridge to understanding, and acknowledgment, if not unconditional acceptance.

As editor, I make no apologies to those who may find parts of this anthology crude, or offensive. If my role was to hold up a mirror and reflect a generation, I had to do so with integrity, without masking anything I or anyone else might disagree with or find objectionable. Reality is not an act of consensus. Nothing was gratuitously included in this anthology because it came across as outrageous or provoking. Every poem in this book is representative of a whole set of poems among the thousands that were submitted.

Finally, I want to acknowledge and thank from my heart the hundreds of poets from around the world who worked with me to gather this collection. This book is much more theirs than mine. And my admiration goes out to all those who had the courage to share pieces of such personal self-expression, knowing they might be exposing themselves to ridicule and rejection. That may be the strongest hope of your generation, that willingness to speak out important issues, rather than burying them deep from the light of day, never to find discussion, dialogue, and resolution. Also, I thank all of you for accepting my thirst to understand who you are, even though I am not of your generation. You have quenched my desire to learn that we aren't really so different after all, that we share in so much more than our ages might separate us.

marlow peerse weaver

POEMS and POETS (in order of appearance)

Talkin' `bout my G-G-G-G-G-Generation

A woman tells me I am the voice
of my generation
and I laugh.

My generation has no voice
and a thousand voices
at once, I tell her.

I tell her:

My generation did not have Woodstock.
We had the Persian Gulf,
Baywatch Beach Party,
Pamela Anderson's manufactured breasts
bobbing in time to the <u>drum `n' base</u>
of Patriot missiles.

My generation had presidents who got into office
by taking hostages.
We had the cold war.
We grew up wearing coats,
fearing the color red.

We had glam rock.
We had new wave, growing old
in the eighties, the politics of dancing,
the alternative
of a shotgun to the head.

By the time we were born, dada
was dead. We were post post
modern kids cutting our teeth
on The Superfriends and Jolt Cola,
latch-key kids in a sugar rush
waiting for mom to pop a t.v. dinner
into the microwave.

My generation is so comfortable with the idea
of annihilation
that we nuke our food.

My generation jumps
from trend to trend, so new,
so retro.

Poetry, for my generation
was a two month fad
on MTV, the revolution televised,
homogenized, and satirized.

My generation is a conglomerate, corporate
marketing effort.

I am not the voice of my generation.
I am the voice of no one
but myself.

C. C. Russell
Wheatland, WY, USA

Friend

My friend I know
you'll read this not
yet pen and paper
will me on
I've thought, at length,
of late on you
your cheerful face
and rakish style
your choice of life and fate.

I'm told at times you
talked to cows
and danced in fields
and cried at rain
a poet's passion
lived in you
no compromise
for things askew.

did you, then, too
when but a boy
dream of ships
and open seas
of righting wrongs
and facing down
Armadas of the Tyranny.

with rapier wit
and cunning laugh
you cut a swathe
through "9 to 5"
unfettered by
convention's chains
young and free and
quite alive.

society, for shame;
it hates
its buccaneering youth
and would just make
us galley slaves till we're
long in the tooth
how gladly did
we go to arms to
fight to free our lives.
from others, knowing better;
Teachers, Priests, Policemen, Wives.

Yet one by one as
life went on
our dreams fell, lost
to the system's guns
and though they never
found their mark
on you,
they struck
the ones you loved.

So in the end
age caught us up
our brief rebellion floundered
They boarded us.
harsh truths their
troops, and viciously, they hounded
then offered up their
terms as such
"conform with no
alternative!" to
live land-locked
in working hell
to question not,
but to obey.
To vote,
But never have a say.

Then you
my buccaneering friend
smiled as the scene grew grim
and raised your flag
with green Doc's on
not waiting for the
coming tide
hoisted yourself
and sailed away
beyond the horizon of mortality.

Ragellion , age 28
Kuraby, Queensland, Australia

Night of Pain

Strange is the night
When the sky is crying
Silent lies the wolf
In the high green grass
Cold is the wind
Coming in from the sea
Dark are the shadows
Creeping on from behind
Angry runs the river
Through the night of pain
And slowly my heart falls asleep
Screaming out it's anger
In the dark wild night
Where I lie next to the wolf

Robert Stenerhag
Örebro, Sweden

Consumer, Consumed

Sarah (frosting heartburn lips,
  greasily skimming hamburger hair)
    looks truer under gumwrapper reflection
    than the rows of zodiac XXXmas
  mirrors competing for credit can show:
Two blue intuitive slippery fish
  snap shut, not showing anybody
    anything but gold, shrouding
      down deep pocket gloat.
    Sarah (hideous Siren shitspitting
    spew or your silicone
    glowing Sunday mother)
is always stacked (in ink) and thinking:
"english cigarettes or library privilege?"
  Still driving by nighttime motel signs
  wishing against finishing
    sold out and old

Sarah Stewart
Peoria, IL, USA

AUTUMN OF DAMNATION

THE LEAVES OUTSIDE MY
WINDOW ARE STARTING TO TURN
AND THE SUN PAVES ETHEREAL
ROADS WITH GOLDEN AFTERNOONS.
THE YEAR'S DYING FASTER
THAN IT WAS BORN,
IT'S ZOOMING WILLINGLY
INTO ITS OWN DEMISE, SEEKING
PEACE IN SILENT FINALITY.
AND I FEEL RIVERS EMPTYING
INTO CHURNING, WRITHING OCEANS,
GEESE'S WINGS PULSING
INSTINCTIVELY FOR FLIGHT,
NORTH WINDS WHIRLING
LIQUID ATOMS INTO ICY FLAKES,
LITTLE FURRY CREATURES BURROWING
INTO THE EARTH, HOARDING FOOD,
BUT MY FEET ARE ENCASED IN
BLOCKS OF WHITE CEMENT,
AND MY HANDS ARE BOUND
WITH PUPPET STRINGS.
I SIT HELPLESSLY, WATCHING TIME
BLOOM AND UNFOLD, TURNING
THE LEAVES OUTSIDE MY WINDOW
AS TIDES RISE AND FALL,
AND GEESE FLY SOUTHWARD
IN SYMMETRICAL V-FORMATIONS
WHILE RABBITS DIG DEEPER
I WAIT FOR LIFE TO TOUCH
ME AS I BECOME MORE DEAF
FROM THE INCESSANT TICKING
THAT SOUNDS LIKE SHORT,
LOUD EXPLOSIONS IN MY HEAD.

"a child of a child of desperation - one with a dead-end job, a dying
father, dying faith, and failing time"

Annepely P. Dakay-Liquigan
Irving, TX, USA

THE RIDE

I'VE BEEN LOITERING AGAIN,
OVER HILLS AND VALLEYS;
OF MY OWN CREATION.
I WANDER...
OVER THE BLUE WATERS OF THE OCEAN,
UNTOUCHED BY STORM OR GALE;
OVER SWAYING PALM TREES,
WHICH SHELTER THOSE WINGED CROONERS.
I WANDER...
OVER MANGROVE SWAMPS,
WHEREIN DWELLS DEATH IN HIDING.
OVER PEAKS AND RIDGES
WHICH ASTOUND THE BRAVEST;
OVER FIRS AND BIRCHES,
WHICH CRAVE TO REACH THE STARS.
AT NIGHT I RIDE THE CRESCENT MOON,
FROM ONE END OF THE HORIZON TO THE OTHER
I FLIRT WITH THE LUMINOUS STARS;
AS I PASS THEM BY.

YET I AM NO WINGED BIRD,
NOR DO I POSSESS MAN-MADE WINGS;
I AM JUST A RIDER,
IN THE CHARIOT OF MY DREAMS.

Murli Menon
Ahmedabad, India

sometimes when the sun
is just over the mountains
and a cloud saves me from
blindness because of my
moth-like attraction
a thin orange border
empties my attention such
that sun cloud mountain
color and I seem one

Simon Damberger
Berthoud, CO, USA

Insignificantly yours:

I thought about the letter that you wrote to me,
Its pages were frayed and spotted with tiny blue swirls,
Where the ink had. . .
As I read it, it occurred to me that I had traded my heart,
Everything I had to offer,
for these few scraps of paper in my hand
As if love is a commodity,
A plaque or a gold watch for faithful service,
A contractual obligation which requires a notice to quit.
I remember not that you left without saying goodbye,
But instead,
That I was worth no more than three pieces of tattered paper
Stuffed inside an envelope and scotch taped to my front door.

"Separations are never easy...
    each of us has a responsibility to grant our partners dignity"

Brandon Hunter
Cornelius, NC, USA

I Can See You Dying

i see you sitting there all drawn up inside.
i can see you melting away.
i feel you inside crying.
i can tell.
It's no secret you're dying.
by the way you glare into unknown worlds,
and seek the truth in people.
you are ready to face death,
as it sees you everyday.
it smacks you on the back,
and says,
" I'll see ya soon"
Then, instead of running,
you answer,
"I am ready to face my doom."
So, now you have your chance.
To do your little dance.
and when you go,
be kind,
and give me a glance.

"written about a friend, who is deathly sick"

★Glitter★, age 16
Weston, WV, USA

Lightness in opposition to heaviness
releases the drenched claustrophobic blanket of searing pain.
The hurt of the lies, the deeply ploughed existence of heartbreak
begins to take root in a new multi-leaved blossom of opportunity.
A flower petalled in bright yellow-orange
emanates a stillness; a completeness bound together
by the thick green stem of battling belief.
A sacred canon of matters profane
giving rise to fun-filled, sun-filled joy.
My blanket dries a mottled hue of bright colours
each and all promising something new and something bigger, better, bolder
a new ray of hope to confront the new days.
A life of love, trust, faith and most of all truth.

"the recovery process begins, though heartache still prevails"

Gavin R. Baker
KwaZulu / Natal, South Africa

School of Poetry

Artsy professors gather around
bohemian coffee shops
gargling out well-written innocuous, politically correct poems
about their Sabbaticals, their maple trees,
sunset views from the Ivory Tower
They bathe anthologies with their spit.
while trying to catch glimpses of eternity
through their Coke bottle spectacles.
They look towards the sky
pondering the symbolism of bird shit.

Not aware they have failed to see:
the sparkling bubbles
in their bottles of soda. . .
icicles hanging from a rusty shed. . .
or words on a page torn from the world. . .
bringing music to scattered houses.
far from those depthless voices
trying to find the patient jewel

away from its own setting.

"many academic journals seems to be vanity presses for English professors"

Marie Griffin
Spartanburg, SC, USA

one night stand (extended)

with every smile
you painted picassos
in my soul
and your body
wrote poetry
between my thighs

for two years

as you left
you saw my tears
and asked
did i really
mean so much
to you

why

"some long-term relationships are only
as meaningful as one-night encounters"

Yvonne Eve Walus
Auckland, New Zealand

The Lovers

He is out of patience. He is young and gray.
He will make his money, up, up and away.

I will write letters to him, send him my love.
I will travel and keep busy, over and above.

He will play with the children, grow grave and fond.
He will hang tire swings, above and beyond.

I will leave the guests for a few minutes and hide.
I will pretend to go shopping, far and wide.

It will not make any sense. It will not be fair.
But we will stay together, here and there.

Sarah Ruden
Baltimore, MD, USA

DANSE DU VENTRE

It is the mind awaiting sunlight,
La horrida bella tempo,
El maestro su es tempo,

In the rubric of his tempo
All the buglers splayed the cento,
In the grand Cochisean drums
A chieftain cuckolds in suspension,
"'tis amour ill fait du jour!"

Parting trumpets, brazen singing
Rifts of paradigm's beginnings
Dark aubades of Latin hymning;
"Liberty, sweet liberty!

It is the ego's dream of conquest, ex effectu or pompous,"
Gesundheit!
"It is the mind awaiting sunlight, lumen naturae turned violent"
(applause)

Or merely fish eyes, snails and motifs
Shuffling sideways to life's fodder
Grist mercurial for daughters whose
Parting songs for parting knaves
Chime a zodiac of wails.

Now a thunderous mandala
Allemandes across its border
Keels a stately polonaise to a
Twitch whose rhythmic shakes
Leads a soft-shoe down its grave.

"the dance of war"

David Hunter Sutherland
Fishkill, NY, USA

LET'S EXPLODE!

I was bursting to say
 that I couldn't hide it.
There's a world out there
 and we're inside it.
Let's not speak
Or think in code.
 Hold your breath-
Let's explode!

Suicides let it out
 and manics hold it in.
Other people thank the Lord
 and choke eternal sin.
Let's not preach.
The vision showed.
 Hold your breath-
Let's explode!

Now we could die on life support
 enslaved to a machine
or we could stare at quantities
 and wonder what they mean.
Let's not preach.
The vision showed.
 Hold your breath-
Let's explode!

If you breathed in and waited you're sad.
 If you breathed out and waited you're tragic.
The beat is as great as it used to be
 if you believe in magic.
Let's not scream out
Or heave our load.
 Hold your breath-
Let's explode!

Evens and odds don't balance out.
 Opposites attract.
Conventional freaks and hippies clash.
 Logic isn't fact.
Let's re-charge
The antipode.
 Hold you breath-
Let's explode!

The sound of music is a sound.
 The setting is a place.
The beauty of the melody
 is like the numb man's face.
Hold your breath.
We're almost gone.
Close your eyes-
Let's carry on.

"the absolute in pop art is the slogan...when a slogan provokes thought without tempting to convince, it might be called poetry"

Yael Sanders
Cote Saint Luc, Quebec, Canada

On hearing Louise G. speculate,
War is men's version of dressing up.

I don't have time to contend every
bone-head philosophy, but
thinking of my grandfather, losing blood
in his legs as his plane spins, spins
down on the long gun-bristling millipede
of a train, and the terrible race
between him and his sweaty swastika-ed
targets, who swung platform guns skyward,
or my cousin, lost for two days
in the bloodbath jungle which crossed many countries,
and the skinny young man
whom he shot in the face as he rose
dreamlike out of long-grass
or my uncle, blackfaced and sloshing
out of night shallows, a backpack full
of explosives strapped to him,
I suspect, pretty uniforms aside,
war is war,
often but not always undertaken,
when a people become tired
of being shot, starved, beaten,
or exhausted with witness.

R. J. McCaffery
Providence, RI, USA

(from ꜰarewell*)*   *(transl. Vyt Bakaitis)*

on leaving ꜰurmala our pockets carry
sand, and we suddenly start our lament for
the past summer, as if it had been discarded
with the silver spoon and fading
flowers dried out in an old volume

will ꜰ be gone from you long? ꜰ'm not sure, except to say
that the shadow of vanished continents will never cease
to guide me, even out there, the homes where love has been
and comets fell like bees on a hive at dusk

*"Language remains one of the most basic of human homes, preserving for us
childhood, our desires and choices, values and ideas, ultimately to define us by
freeing us from time and to release us from isolation by giving us shelter"*

Julius Keleras
New York, NY, USA / Vilnius, Lithuania

Ode to a Short Man

I met a fool just then
A boy, posing as a man,
Who thought he, this package,
Could move, shake me, this wreckage.

It's true I contradict
But all I say is true.

Truly you are a fool
Foolishly think you'd unravel
What only flies free
Free of rulers, including fools.

Quite narrow of you indeed
Unaware of all
I've seen and past deeds.

And it is true
A tidal wave irons a ripple flat.

You seem quite small
To imagine yourself tall.
Tall enough to attempt
Even try the feat at all.

V. Holden
Houston, TX, USA

Pandora

I am content
Then why lament
This passive gladness
This must be madness!
Yet I wonder - if
Happiness has left me bored
stiff
And so I pine
For this angst of mine
Or is it -
Simply a visit
From my contrary mind
That seeks to find
A subject to grope
Other than hope.

*"Why is it that when all seems to go
so well there is something inside that
yearns for conflict?"*

Gila Monster
Montreal, Quebec, Canada

Subtle Escape

*The lonely mind
gets lonelier soon
to go behind
a mystery tune
and hide a day
from the world astray,
think in that tune
a thought that'll sway
a restless hand
to scribble away.*

Arsalan Daudi
Karachi, Pakistan

On the streets

On the streets
truth runs thicker than blood
and faster than runaways
threatened with home
reality is a faceless agony
that chases you down
and leaves you alone
with baby-faced widows
like weather-beaten orphans
who dangle false promises
from windows, like laundry
and tie their shoes
with rubber bands to their feet
and no one ever notices
on the streets

The voice of wishful victory
holds little conviction
though it knows it exists
somewhere- just not here
and opportunity clanks
like a can on a table
and lies flat like a week old beer
lies like the cheap little girl
who sells her soul for a dollar
lies flat
like the old man nobody bothers
we just walk by and lift our feet
'cause you just don't step on
someone who's already
on the street

And time is the hand
that sells you your fix
it doesn't care where it's taking you
it only names its price
and if you spend enough time here
you start feeling like
the world's sacrifice
bound by twisted glory
falling through the shattered ice
of your own vain assumptions
so wrapped in warped expectation
you refuse to see
that there's nothing but
willing victims and cold heat
on the streets

Natasha Jones
Parsonsburg, MD, USA

Shrimp

I'm not really allergic to shellfish.
I just didn't want to go to that restaurant
cause I used to fuck the bartender there
and you don't look as good as him
and I don't look as good as I did then
and he would notice that
and go home and tell the guy he lives with,
the guy that always thought I was a slut.
So I guess that means we won't be
spending eternity together because
I could never tell you that and
I'm not willing to give up shrimp for you.

Jennifer Leanne Waller
Jonesboro, GA, USA

LET ME OUT

Let me out of this stifling room
filled with anguish and despair
Give me wings so that I can fly
And give me courage so that I'd dare

Let me soar in the highest sky
away from torment and distress
To catch the wind to a foreign land
To live my life in the absence of press

To live in freedom without this pain
that tears me down, day by day
Let me out before it's too late
That's all I ask for, that's all I pray

Peter Engholm
Melbourne, Australia / Trelleborg, Sweden

Lightning

We
are our own worst habit
keep trying to kick ourselves,
keep finding ourselves
marooned with moronic questions:
if you could choose your own death...
would you rather be
deaf or blind?
If you could go back in time,
kill Napolean, Hitler...Reagan?
asked to plan the
circumstances surrounding
a stranded-on-a-desert-island-bring-one-whatever-with-you
daydream.
Deserve better than this we keep saying,
our name on a marquis in medium type,
someone to stir our martinis,
give our pinkies a little credit for knowing where the tab key is.
We haven't forgotten how to reciprocate.
We might be castaways,
but we got our morals in zeroed-in,
we know just what we'd do if we could
hone in our cross-hairs.
Just give us a chance instead of
the party-favor chatter.
A hair-trigger query into our preference of
inconvenient handicaps.
We got 20/20 pessimism
and contacts,
a stylish drug problem and health food,
jock itch and the nasty attitude to prove it.
We got passionless scorn balancing
doggie-treat on the tip
of our academic noses,
our pretence pulled tight
our eyes wide and
our zippers
loose.
but, this is not the death we choose.
If you really must inquire,
we divide our disdain evenly between
"in my sleep" and the guys who want to die
by orgasm-heart-attack.
"Why such mediocre dreams," we scream.
"Have ye no vision?!"

We want to die by
lightning bolt!

We want death to race
down a
bright-yellow cartoon staircase.
We're gonna fry.
We want to die extra-crispy.
We want to show our bones
in filament afterglow.
to hear our own viscera sizzle
to smell the cremation of every memory exploding at once.
The watches we keep in
top
dresser
drawers
proof of time well spent
living with weirdos and their odd socks.
Our alliances based on similar selection
of independent
bumper stickers.
We're ready for every twitchable, switchable, signal-sendable cell
from our toes to tongue to tits & testicles to
flex as it has never flexed before.
An orgasm-heart-attack stronger than
any man or woman could dream to deliver.
Sure,
there's dirt in our other pair of jeans
we don't talk about,
sometimes intense cookie crumbs in the pockets.
We don't have time for
this season's fashionless fashion:
Guys in big black shoes,
girls in small black underwear
no
lace.

We're gonna be frayed and snagged,
feel the surge run up our backs,
have our souls snatched away so fast
our bodies sonic-boom as they slam back together.
a fate untouchable
by murder or suicide.
We'll stand taller than anything for miles.
The trees will thank the heavens for the lightning-rod
of our sacrifice.
We will call down fire and watch the sky obey.
and one day
the prophets will say that their gods could not suffer us to live
for even another
instant.

Jon Williams
Raleigh, NC, USA

In Which Here I Turn

the world has trapped me in its turn,
i fear it,
but me to it is no concern.

me, so unimportant
and small
trapped in a huge world
that knows all.

will a mark i hope to make some day
really change such a mass
in any big way?

i am nothing really,
but a speck of dust,
with some feelings,
as love and lust,

but to the world in which here i turn,

this is not to its concern.

"I often feel meaningless and unimportant
in this massive world I live in"

Laura Theodorow, age 16
St. Charles, MO, USA

Flowers in the Field

Sunshine speckled
green grass beauties
in amongst the weeds and grey
The flowers shine on a
lighter way,
glowing through despair
they reach for the light.

Amanda Closson
Canada

"Who Am I?"

A lost child,
chasing his youth.
Trying to discover the mysteries,
that lie behind the eyes,
that stare at him in the mirror.

Jim Healey, age 26
Cleveland, OH, USA

Without You

In autumn,
when the torches burn
in the temples of Mei,
I find myself beside you.

Your lips,
your eyes,
these things I miss.

Your hair
brushing softly
against my sun-burned cheek.

Your smile,
spread wide for the world
to glimpse through,
enlightens me.

I see you
no other way,
but truly,
a person of many lives.

Your kind words
reached even the depths
of my confusion.

Your pity, though no longer needed,
was such
that I could not scorn it,
though I am proud.

Your voice lies for me
at the bottom of an endless well,
so that I,
seeking it,
cease to breathe the air.

Instead,
I sink deeper
into the waters,
the waters of your soul.

Far away,
beyond the walls
and valleys of Mei,
you lay
undisturbed
by my grieving thoughts.

I would that I,
not frightened by your intensity
anymore,
but with a love true,
could find
that place you dwell in.

For I am in the darkness
without you.

"if asked, I shall say that I belong to you, though you have left"

Faith , *age 18*
Los Angeles, CA, USA

The word on you is simple - that you're nuts,
Supported by words of heady scorn.
I think I'd like to see those crazy eyes,
Beside my pillow in unhurried morn.

The question is only one of guts
And whether on the way we dare and win
Or let the morning light look over
A bed of chastity, not sin

So if you're nuts, be nuts for me,
And let the world laugh off this pair:
He dances in the moonlight, showing off,
His ecstaextra eyes and deep blue hair

While she, expecting nothing, only pines
For love to swing in on some jungle vines.

Dena Bugel-Shunra
Tel-Aviv, Israel

SeaSOn Of eMoTiOnS

in the cold of Winter we met
seasonably happy
was I when you came my way

now Spring, yield yet
showers of your affections
in which, I bathe myself each day

but Summer, brought
stormy moments
our tears poured down like rain

so by Autumn, never married
we fell apart
like leaves that brown, our hearts did change

Eric Anthony Brown - "Oyaji"
Honolulu, HI, USA

Bone day

That day
when your death became reality
touchable like my very own flesh

That day
the sky wept

The sorrow of five long years
came bursting out
hitting me
again and again

What was this sorrow
my own solitude
my own sense of loss?

Can't avoid
the terror
the fear
I embrace it
love it
at the peak
of the emotion

The day they found you
I dressed in white
my black tears
rolling down
like grapes
until transparent
I knew by then
I was healed

The movement of denied feelings
making me
lighter
stronger
brighter
as I sang out
all your names
in a current of sad joy

The day they found you
I dressed in white
my eyes
shining
with the whole emotional scale
my voice
transforming
from hurt to healing

The day they found your
weathered bones
I dressed in white
watered my plants
of sorrow
with my tears of joy

"My husband's body was found after being lost for 5 years, the 17th of June 1998.
I wrote this poem the day I was informed that the bones belonged to him"

May the sun walk with you,
    the moon smile to you.
Walking the milky way
you might look down and
throw a star towards me.
To remind me there is more.
Much more then our eyesight can grasp.
May you be what you are and will always be.
A delicate being with heart-shaped hands of light.

Birgitta Jonsdottir, age 31
Reykjavik, Iceland

Where are the humans?

They say there are now six billion humans.
Yet I see none,
Save self-illuminating suns
And caviar-dense congregations
Spread over the sweet crust of custom.

Ilias Chrissochoidis
Stanford, CA, USA

Fine Line

There's a fine line between you and I
between the earth and sky
and how and why we live and die
Between you and me what you hear and what you see
between the end and endlessly
between the chance and guarantee
Two sides of one mind
what's a sin and what's a crime
what you lose and what you find
too much and not enough time

It's a fine line There's a fine line
It's a fine line There's a fine line
cross that fine line and slip into my mind

Between us and them
between once and once again
reality and what's pretend
between the start and bitter end
Between Heaven and Hell
what you think and what you tell
if you're pushed or if you fell
between the wish and wishing well
Between caught and free
agony and ecstasy
between half full and half empty
to be alone or be lonely
between close and far
from here to the nearest star
losing control and taking charge
and knowing when you've gone too far

Karen Kenedy
Colorado Springs, CO, USA

Beyond white's silence
Closed, now opens to wide sky
Spectrum of light flies

"a senyru inspired by a Ng Ken Liong photograph"

Kucinta Setia
Republic of Singapore

being an x-er is about disappointing those before.
the boomers, those sad fucking sell outs,
can't understand why I and my friends don't want their sad utopia,
which is just a warped, mangled vision
of the utopia of their parents
and their parents' parents.
they took power from those who went before them
and became just like them.
so they're disappointed when we reject their values.
fuck them! i don't want their
sad middle class dreams
in a world of poverty and strife.
i don't want their talk of peace and love
when all they deliver is greed, war and chaos.
i don't want their values
in a world where we're numbers on a balance sheet.
i don't want their high talk
of standing for what you believe in
when they dumped their free love, peace and understanding
and jumped on the treadmill to make a quick buck
and have become as conservative
and unchanging
as those before them.
most of all,
i don't want their fucking label,
their "x" tag that's meant to define me,
put me neatly in a little box,
sum me up in a letter of the alphabet.
my generation is an accident of timing,
an error of birth,
born with the bad luck
to be in a world
fucked up by the generation before the boomers,
and made worse by the "children of aquarius"
when they took the reins.

"baby boomers complain endlessly about the `Generation X' as unmotivated, undisciplined, etc...a bit rich coming from the generation that reveled in the `Greed is Good' 80's and whose talk of revolution and societal change was just that, talk"

Mike Augustin
Perth, Western Australia

("cyclic artists")

there will be many of us left when we die,
strangling in empty thought,
dipping drowned head in stars
that are only black helicopters, fingering
ourselves for revelations that
fill us & dissipate into animal-urge,
simmered in olive oil & garlic
of the warm home trap, loving killing
hating trusting every lie on television,
believing so hard that we smash
our own pieces of paradise, freeing
the blinded masses from our silent
brick & brain cages;
smoking resin begging each other for purpose
talking late into the morning so many voices
when ours is gone.

Christina Gay
Baltimore, MD, USA

Poetic license where no driver's one exists

Sitting in solitude on this moving institution
Sixty cents to have an hour with me and my pen
My God as my inspiration.
Hours, days, in quiet solitude on this
Mass transportation.
Ideas, like rivers flow through my soul
With no where to go, except the pen.
And the paper.
Hours, days of my life just searching
The depths of my soul.
Excuse my bluntness,
but this is my present to life, who has
Given me so much
This is my voice in the void.
These are my views and loves,
And my hates.
My joys and my sadness.
This is my trip, home from school.
Tired, but the pen calls, and I must answer.
To know me is to read
One hour's worth of what
I write on this bus.
This gift from heaven,
That I give on.

"I write all my poetry on Jacksonville buses"

Michelle Meux, age 19
Jacksonville, Florida, USA

SHE IS A BIRD
(transl. Bert Meelker)

Poem for Lorraine Williams

She is a bird
traveling among the clouds
dropping in every country
a unique piece of herself
that is the solitude accompanying her
sprouting love
in seeds without sire
in foreign lands.
She is a bird
free in the heavenly space
without fear of going up or going down
and without child that can die.
She is a post-modern bird
that lives together with the comets
just like the poets
on cold days,
and when she goes away
the rainbow seems empty
and turns grey
like the city of London.
William Shakespeare
was keeping me company
and brought his love poems,
and the Hundred Year War
settled itself in me,
inside my chest
and despite this I decided to breathe.
It seems that the English language
that never suited me well
and that I never learned
decided to trouble me
and show me the word love
that I could feel completely
without ever properly understanding it.

She is a bird
and I left the window open
and suddenly she disappeared,
and my gaze grew old seeing her leave.
She is a bird
and I know not in what place
she may be today,
I only know that when I look at the sky
I know that there should be stars
just like she should be
in some part of the sky of this planet,
and I feel a longing
that seems to have made the stars
numb and extinguished to me.

Cristiane Neder
Sao Paulo, Brazil

Listless

Turning away from our ignorance
Waiting to be saved
Making it known that we won't walk
Until our path has been paved.
Pretending we lack the willpower
To make up our own choices;
We struggle to accomplish nothing
And make no use of our voices.

"the stubbornness of my generation and the ignorance we submerge ourselves into to avoid reality is getting us nowhere"

Amy Sutterer, age 15
Cedar Falls, IA, USA

Verbs with such meaning

In this life I have many things to give,
But more I want to take.
I see,
I feel,
But not like this.
A piece of dialogue I remember,
Made no sense.
But was absolute in the circumstance.
My memories, rush forth and cry.
Some in Joy.
Some in Anger.
I need to feel,
To think,
To touch,
To Be.
Verbs with such meaning.
I need to love,
Be loved.
I have done these things before,
And yet a blur passes through
As I speak.
My stomach clenches.
It's not real.
I'm on my knees:
Feeling weak.

"I sometimes feel the physicality of emotions, the credibility of words has been lost and replaced by something less meaningful"

Linzi Harvey, age 16
Southampton, Hants, England

the hipster's heartburn

what is cool?
cool is what?
cool is cool
cool is knowing mingus and what mingus is
cool is wanting to know mingus when not knowing what mingus is
cool is cunnilingus with fellatio
double dipped ice-cream cone
a sunny disposition with a cool breeze
in your face the trails to knowledge
broken roads of time placed like indentation's fingerprints
DNA, cells, ameba, parasites, dirt, water, air
cool is individuality born of itself
the person who is you, distinguished from me
knowing whom one must be in the journey
life is cool
cool like a crisp river by the forest
cool like the old black man and indian sitting on stoop of barbershop
cool is the long stride in a woman's strut
the muscles in mama's thigh, something not thought out loud
and the men all pause in space
bend down to pick up things not lost
cool is one more try to spectacular
all or nothing to lose, like a devastating desire
to become that dream once dreamt
to become the world all at once
to be humble in that moment, is cool
to be humble, modest, serene
to be assured, honest, loveable
to be a man, woman, human
to be all at once and nothing at all
cool is the eye that sees when closed
the breath felt on the neck from your lover
the smell of a baby, the sound of its lungs/ exploding
cool is another chance at the dream
cool is to dream the dream
what is the dream? cool
bury the hatchet in that jazzy groove
cool it out, baby
and cool will be a hot sauce
you pour on all you consume

"cool is those things tangible to us, around us, and in us"

Curtis L. Crisler
Fort Wayne, IN, USA

We took turns at holding the knife

We took turns at holding the knife
Like two players from Westside.

You acted the liberated woman,
I made my exit as the graceless
Fay Weldon man.

But you held the knife first, making you the prime culprit my dear
Because, as you once explained to me,
Playground rules never disappear, they just hide in the thickets
Of our pubic hair.

We held hands under the victory phallus, the high zest of Trafalgar Square.
Your heat traveled. A wave changing left-of-stage into a particle.
An illegal lodger, snug as a bullet, in the squalid housing of my build.

The birthday watch (your delicately inscribed gift) screamed in alarm,
Waking me from a pleasant yet somehow tainted
Afternoon. The look in your eyes told me that
Soon, very soon, a role reversal was to take place.
I felt a tide surging from my non existent womb,
As I pleaded, Dido-like, for your Aeneas heart.
It was too late, we were too close to the finishing line
For another start. And you my dear were through
With your game of debauch and depart.

We think of chance as a creature of spiky persuasion.
A fleeting shooting star, a once in a lifetime affair.
Yet being the daughter of randomness, having that chaotic lineage,
Means that chance is often an actor in a small production,
Forced to stage many guises.
So when you rang that time-mid-November-hungering
For our last Christmas lights, I should have felt the tide turning,
I should have listened to my heart. No devil handed the knife.
No death pushed no cursed cart. I made the plunge, I forced the dart
And held you, a wounded Echo, across the telephone line.

We took turns at holding the knife.
Our pride took care of the rest.

Hassan Abdulrazzak
New Malden, Surrey, England

Feminism

I want you to have a lot to say;
I want it all to be about me.
Remember how I cleaned my house?
That was me, dammit; I'm clean now.
My cobwebs are gone. Uncluttered.
I cut my hair not too long ago.
Can you see my face better now?
You say you want me, but that isn't enough.
How do you want me? How often? How long?
I want you to be dirty and perverse.
Tell me how beautiful I'd look in lingerie.
Describe to me my ass when I walk.
Try to explain the little things I do that turn you on.
Write me anxious sexy poems;
tell me romantic twisted tales.
Let me be your first at something.
Tell me everything about your past
that you wish you didn't remember.
I can be your counselor.
Redecorate your eyes to see my face.
Accept me. Let me be over the top.
I'll suck the consequences.

Laura A. Fletcher
Morgantown, WV, USA

i'll catch that arrow
from the golden bow of love
pierce it if i must
into your heart for the god
of love missed you when he shot

from "Leaves of Tanka"

Santiago B. Villafania
Manila, Philippines

PONDERING INSANITY

Rocking back and forth
Arms around my knees
Swaying to the music
Of terminal disease
Wander through my head
Thoughts I shouldn't think
Dangle over madness
Wobble on the brink
Blurry kinds of people
Images of stone
Flowerpots are empty
I am all alone
Hearing sounds of torture
Spilling from the walls
Corridors of time
Left as empty halls
Pictures hung around
Laughter in my head
Round and round my brain cells
Wish that I was dead
Memories in the mirror
Rusted silver chain
Little songs and poems
Driving me insane
Darkness is invading
Pillows on my bed
Dear, say your last goodnight
Whispers in my head
Gremlins in a nightmare
Flight of golden stairs
Pondering insanity
Darling, say your prayers.

"written at 2 in the morning, psychotic ramblings that came raw from my wandering mind"

Leslie Wolos
St. Francois Xavier, Manitoba, Canada

MATERIAL WORTH

IN MY STRUGGLE TO BECOME SOMEONE
I LOST MYSELF
IN MY BID TO BE WEALTHY
I "SOLD" EVERYTHING VALUABLE
IN MY SEARCH FOR HAPPINESS
I RELINQUISHED MY SMILE.

Kelly Pilgrim
Southern River, WA, Australia

chemistry x geometry = you + me

i am a triangle. me and me and me
took a poll this morning -- tried to
agree on who is obtuse who is acute and
who is right. i am. a fulcrum found
beneath all that teeter-totter mish-mash.
i want to settle in balance but upside-down me
yields to whimsical tenets -- oddly opposite but
connected we three.

he is a circle. o, he thinks i fit so perfectly
into his wholly self -- his fond arms around
all-angled me. he is. a tire that rolls
sync-smooth but triangle me lies ever so tangent --
gotta have radial symmetry. patient -- he triumphs some --
but i wanna get around.

if i could cut across his middle --
leaving room for me me and me on
all my sides where we don't fight and
equal i -- congruency -- enfold all
trust to diametrical he...i think
i'd have to force us into wound-weakened
foreign area -- i fear a noose if i
mettle in we. i'm the girl out in
trifle town afraid it'll all crash.

if it were just you me and chemistry
we'd metamorph and correspond.
but we're just trite realms in geometry. so --
say -- ya know any single squares
lookin' for a diagonal?
i've got a free side.

Heather L. Igert
St. Louis, MO, USA

Couplet Dance

*We danced so hard, feet stomping, crashing down
like mama dinosaurs cracking the earth.
Disheveled hair jumping on our shoulders
lifting in ignorance of gravity.
Gazing upward with gaping mouths like blind
saltwater fish searching for lost sunrays.*

Elizabeth Germanio
Cincinnati, OH, USA

We

And if we are beat,
and if we embody paradox,
then at least
we are inevitable,
and can clam to sleep
in our inevitabilities.
And if their seeds are our birthmarks,
Rage to revitalize the dead tongues;
make them our own.
And if we are again
shunned back into the chute status
of Subterannia,
Yet are minimum wage suburbanites
hooked on heroin and boredom,
mammaling security from our
swooshes and stripes,
waving a drought flag
of nonconformity,
and bargaining for
who knows what,
then what of our favorite teddy bears?
And if to think aloud is expected
and response responsibilities are tongued
to us,
why do the "evolved"
still nose us like cheerleaders
in drag,
on drugs,
and singing sweetly to seduce
a drunken moon.
And if we are destined to
rival every old rivalry
that's grown so traditionally
stale
that we couldn't tell it's been
rivaled before,
no voices, no vices.
We stop-
-four-way stop sign;
spinning,
submissing to our amnesia
and laying down right
in the heart
of the intersection,

beat and run over
by the power ties
and gauze bazookas,
desperately trying to anew
something
"FUCK" could not.
And in that final frenzy
when we revel in our inevitabilities,
Nostalgia this dismal wind.
And in this moment,
before we fall off the flat
earth,
with our
"who the hell cares what happened in 1492!",
when we scramble
for our spontaneous timecards
and doomed chemistry,
frantically trying to punch out
before we go
overtime,
O let the motion itself be divine.

*"how can we change the world, when we're working weekends at fast food
franchises…how can we aspire to be President, when we can't afford an
education…how can we fight, when we're too beaten down to revolt…we
just watch the television, eat our breakfast cereal, watching the lies unfold,
waiting for the system to collapse"*

George F. Emmerich
Spring Hill, FL, USA

Today

*You died today
and it's true what
they say,
the sun still shines —*

mercilessly

"the day my grandfather died I realised the potential for `endless grief'"

Kelly Pilgrim
Southern River, WA, Australia

Sometimes

It's just another day –
Equally suitable for murder and for prayer,
For one causes the other.

Sometimes I wish that life was more like existence --
Not like a play, where we wear masks
Placed on our faces by our friends,
Who are merely actors like us.
Sometimes I wish an enormous black shadow
Could suddenly hide our faces
From everybody's eyes,
And people were given freedom to imagine
How others look at them when they take off the masks.

Sometimes I wonder
Why people tend to kill each other?
Is it because of personal preferences or self-preservation?
Maybe they don't know what to do with power and wealth?
Or maybe they want to know how accurate their new gun is?
Probably all this -- beginning with curiosity -- is our nature.

And maybe, just maybe –
I could hear the sound of guns
Falling from their hands,
Since the shadows all around
Look too much like their own...
If only such one enormous shadow existed!

I promise I would be the first
To drop my weapon,
And although those around me
Will be hesitant to follow,
I pray that I would be brave enough to put my arms
Around another faceless shadow by my side.

Still, whether I want it or not,
It will be just another day –
Equally suitable for murder and for prayer.

*"dedicated to the participants of the 1987 American-Soviet Peace Walk from
St. Petersburg to Moscow"*

Andrey Y. Morozov
Moscow, ID, USA/St. Petersburg, Russia

girlhood and the lesbian

a state of being that we hold, grasp
tinged and peaked at the sight
of the new york city billboard
with the woman
in the bikini
her hand tauntingly near
tauntingly near the elastic
to pull down and embrace
to clutch the heightened
bone
of sharpened hips.
you kiss these smiling lips so soft
in your girlhood
imagination
of a lesbian affair
tauntingly near
to temptation.

the girl.
the girl who sits on the bench
before the nude woman
and runs a finger down
the decadent curves
touching
the dangling surfaces
she knows
in foreign fantasies
Lady of the Evening
en deshabile.

the girl.
the girl who watches the leaves walking
stumbling down the cobblestone path
into the gutter
where the rainwater
and spilled ice cream mix
to form a pink and mottled mixture
called love.
and breasts that wander down the avenues
striking chords with skyrises
like the selfsame jutting hipbones
of the selfsame jutting love.

that girl.
that girl who reads her poetry
devours and deflowers
her virgin bud
for the pert rhythmic gyration
of a byronic sensation
a byronic fall.
it is the laughter of a million idols
a million whispers
of poppy fields
bleeding red in a flame glow firelight
of a flame glow bleeding heart.

*"at different points in our lives, we come
upon realizations of who and what we are"*

Sara Lampert
Metuchen, NJ, USA

Understanding

now that i am here,

so to speak,

have arrived.

it is
transparently clear,
that
what is vital,

at least for me.

is to

turnaround,
and do
all i can

to get back,
to where i came from.

Jason Smith
Church Crookham, Fleet, England

Tempting Heaven: A Methodist
Meditation Poem on Rwanda

cry do the children cry
who can

unlike fathers and mothers
and farm life memories
rendered roadside deposits
still lives stilled forever
fixed upon foreign films:
modern epitaphs to tragedy.

our hearts are also heavy
holding prayer books
with trembling hands
with the terrible knowledge
of bloody burial pits blowing
decay down the lungs
of the living.

cry do the spirits cry
as I

know it happened again
again came roman legions
again came turkish armies
again came nazi monsters
again came the killing fields
again Cain's curse
has swallowed whole
our wicked words
spat out carnage
tempting heaven
to again cleanse
the world of humanity.

today's war crime charges
today's human rights judges
today's imprisoned killers
today's hung murderers
add little moral weight
to our collective body.

these legal procedures
pale next to a single farmer
born to feed a hungry nation.
they pale further next to
his first son born shivering
in the gentle arms of a nurse
a black bundle of innocent charm
cheated yet challenged
to make his father's land
bear fruit once again.

*"It is not exaggerated to believe our generation will resuscitate this drifting
democracy by combining knowledge of the past with our fears for the future.
Who cares wins."*

Mark Antony Rossi
Jersey City, NJ, USA

TEN YEARS AFTER HIGH SCHOOL

It wasn't San Andreas fault, it wasn't anyone's fault
my graduating class ended up in detox or working
in Gap stores. The earth shook under us no matter
where we went. Our parents ran away to
trailer communities so they could
drive away fast, if need be. They would have said
blame the system, but have you ever tried to

find Mr. Gap? Even the moon could use some
stress management now. Our parents said there was a man
in it, but he's gone

only a worn-out frisbee sighs
down on us, non-biodegradable

us and the various
endings we
graduated into.

"lost innocence, loss of faith, and an absence of humane authority figures"
　　　　　Jeanette Lynes
　　Antigonish, Nova Scotia, Canada

Jeff

Sometimes i wanna pull you up from under the ground...
i just wanna hear your voice to remember the sound...
wanna see your face to make sure you were real...
wanna hold your hand just so i could feel...
wanna kill bloody dreams i have of you at night...
pull you from them to make sure your all right...
wanna forget the sight of you with half a head...
laying in that coffin forever dead...
wanna hold onto the memories of your better dayz...
but all they can do is be re-played...
wanna remember your face but its fading away...
try to hold it in my head but i cant make it stay...
i guess i should be happy coz your better off than me...
...you got set free...
but i cant help but miss you when i look at the ground...
coz i know your laying underneath there...dead as sound...

"in memory of my friend Jeff, who at the age of 16 was shot and killed by his own father...I'll miss him always"
　　　　　Layla Hudgins
　　Arlington, TX, USA

The Bold New Order

Twisted glares from the source of all uneasiness
I ponder ~
> who has learned how to draw the last straw
> without taking all of us down with them?

I crave the times that once were
The lies biting at my ankles all the while
But at least then I was pure to others

I am nothing but what I feared I would always be
Shameful, crooked, lustful and true
How wrong can that be?

Honesty can break you
Lies can cover you
What is the world coming to?

Katie, age 18
Paynesville, MN, USA

POWER OF A DREAM

Once when I was asleep in bed,
And eerie lights enveloped my room and I
A soothing dream then entered my thoughts,
Spreading its wings as time rolled by.

A dream to be remembered,
I imagined I had fulfilled my goal,
With my ambitions all completed,
Steady as the fruits then rolled.

I wondered when I awoke,
If it would someday be a part of my reality
When I would be proud of what I did,
Regardless of what others said to me.

And so in that night, I whispered,
More to myself, I said,
I'd make my valued wish come true,
And stand in dignity where my dream has led

Jingyu Zhao
China

Speechless *(transl. M.P. Weaver)*

There are those
who are speechless
because they're strangers
in a strange land

There are those
who are speechless
because indifference
has cut out their tongue

There are those
who are speechless
because of
      rage
      sadness
      loneliness
      and forlornness

If I am not able to speak
one sensible word with you
then it is not out of
      hate or contempt
towards you

It is simply because

      I'm speechless

"forlornness is an existentialist term meaning `losing religion, fatherland, etc.'"

Nguyen Ngoc Lien
Munich, Germany

LISTEN

listening to the last spark which dimly lights my path
holding back the darkness the embodiment of my wrath
foolishly stepping forward towards something not there
irresponsibly pressing when I do not care
giving false hope, not losing lost respect
It's my inter self that I learn to reject
seclusion drives me to your culpable desire
My ego, not my heart burns of malevolent fire

Michael McNolty
Newton, KS, USA

Felidae

I am not Jane Austen
I have a savanna heart
I won't be cabin'd, cribb'd, confin'd.

To hell with risk
there are claws in couches too
Lilliputian perhaps
but many barbs make sharp dirks.

Pretty gewgaws fascinate
but can't content, the distant scent
of wind stirred grass and pride spawned musk pulls sinews tight.

Keep your pap
your sniveling security, your matching lamps and Laura Ashley shirts
I go to hunt fresh meat.

And when I have savaged the flesh I have found
filled my gut to painful distension
I will crack the bones with a large smooth stone
and suck the delicious pabulum till there's not a globule more.

*"was written in frustration when I was considering leaving job, family,
everyone and everything behind and starting again"*

Joy Reid
Sale, Victoria, Australia

On Each Side of the Shadow

*My mother never really knew her father.
Just a two dimensional figure
with no depth or color.
Just black, and white.
One, or the other.
In her only picture of him, he holds her,
smiling at the life in his arms.
There's white in the button up shirt he wore.*

*Yet there is black of the shadows of his eyes,
When he left her, forgotten.
And when she thought of him,
she saw the closed-lip
smile in the picture.
And she could never tell if his teeth were square pearls,
or black diamonds.*

*"When my mother was a baby, her father ran off to California…the only
remaining memory of him a black and white photo"*

Jon Miller, age 16
Ringoes, NJ, USA

MY CHILDREN

My son,
my daughter;
if ever you may be.
Let me introduce myself: I am your father
and you exist now simply as these thoughts
in my head. But you are more than that,
you will be more than that.
How much more or less we may never know.
I often wonder that if ever you may be,
who will you be? Will you be me?
I could only hope that if not me who you be,
be at least one who can see the pain in others
and the deceit of the world and still
have hope in love, in poetry and in beauty
holding out over the constant grind of
society's reality.
I wish I knew what you would think,
That you would be true to yourselves and your
neighbours.
That you would not fall to the blindness of
egotism, arrogance and the self possession
of materialism.
I hope that you will have the
strength to say no and the wisdom to say yes.
I dream of loving you for who you are
and be given the chance to teach you
in all that you will need to know.
I am proud now of what you can be then.
Because my son, my daughter,
if ever you may be,
you will always be
my Children.

Gregory "Sicarius" Denyes, age 21
Belleville, Ontario, Canada

"Benevolent Correspondence With Winter-Fire! Needfully"

I have spent the cold nights
contorted and whispering on the telephone
until dawn.
Ears bared wide listening
to the shaky voice
on the receiver, trembling in the nuance
of passion, dimmed by the years
and miles, made rusty by the moist bellows of the ocean wind,
wind turning her hair-fire.

These nights laid before me,
like the fallen brothers of addiction
cold, unmoving, spent like the ashes of reefer magic.
They speak fables of godheads chanting,
rhythmic dirge of lament
for wrongs passed, junkless and in love
in the ides of June,
smiling, without trepidation
on the smoke drenched stones, formed in
a staircase, laughing at sexuality and war
with the early minds
that will strike down the world,
and redistribute the sovereignty
of the new beginning
that lies in all.

In the long nights that come
steadfast to the habitual needs,
I've rested, squandering breath
with useless mastication,
speaking treason over my knuckles to
the quivering glow of a cigarette,
lit in remembrance of the lost,
like church candles and tired hate.
And with spilling tendrils of frost
testing the machinery strength of man,
with the binging and purging temperatures
fluxing over the sleeping lives,
above me like the raised fist of unity's strength,
I lived these cold and hollow nights
watching sisters broken under
the backside of man,

tapping my fingers to the walking notes
of distant concertos,
holding rage-fire! in my arms
she falters under the fear of love,
the fear of endless unprotected.
These nights were rimmed and dipped
in the purging sentiment of true love,
with necks lonely and bare.
The moonlight shades the mossy minds of madmen,
deifying the severed head of
innocence rambling, and yet I continue...

Wrapped now in the umbilical wire
from the telephone's split ends of
communication, I sit and count
on the digits of fist-clarity,
the cold nights to the trembling hair-fire,
whittling herself beauty from my whispers.

Sean Casey
Hudson, NY, USA

THE CULMINATION

WHEN ONE TREADS THE VEILED PATH OF DEATH
REMAINS BUT THE FAINT DRIPPING OF THE FEW LAST BREATHS
THOUGHTS INVADE LIKE THUNDER, THE SKY'S SONG
IT'S THEN, THAT ONE REMEMBERS THE PAST
AND ALL THE LOVED, TO THE TICKING CLOCK LOST
THE SWEET SCENT, THE FLOWING HAIR
THE PASSION IN HER EYES, THE LIPS LAID BARE
AND KISSES THAT BURNT LIKE FLARES
THE RAVISHED RUINS, OF LOVE AFFAIRS
STRANGE SPECTRES BECKON THY FRAIL HANDS
THE PUPILS TO AN UNSEEN LIGHT EXPAND
A DROP OF SWEAT ON THE BROW FREEZES INTO AN ISLAND
AS DEATH OF THY FAINT BREATHS TAKES COMMAND
AND SLAYS ONE OF THE LAST THREE THAT STAND
AS WINE IS LOST IN THE DRUNKEN MAN
AS TO THE WIND IS LOST A GRAIN OF SAND
DON'T STRUGGLE, FATE IS LIKE WATER IN YOUR HANDS
SO UNFAIR, THIS GAME OF LIFE AND DEATH
YOU ARE BORN WITHOUT CONSENT, YOU DIE WITHOUT INTENT
ONCE ALL IS RIGHT, THEN IT'S ALL TOO QUIET

Naeem Raza
Lahore, Pakistan

Devoid

Standing at the entrance of a world devoid of pain,
You stood and watched my tears, and said it was the rain.
You spun me round in circles with a cage I could not see,
Then laughed at my frustration with the battle to be free.

I heard you were an echo, weaving fantasy and lies,
A mute bird cannot sing, but you could hear it's cries.
I tried to find a reason, then you piled them at my feet,
I reasoned I was wrong, you were a harsher dream to beat.

I traded dreams for darkness, threw my head into my hands,
Slow motion sparks of wisdom drawing pictures in the sand.
I pointed to the ocean, you called it just a stream,
I touched to find it dry and reality a dream.

You cursed me for the sunlight, I blamed you for the pain,
I couldn't wait around for the sun to rise again.
A fighter never dies and a mute bird can't be heard,
However much I raged you denied I said a word.

I climbed up every mountain, so desperate for a cure,
Stopped the world from turning to keep you where you were.
I tried to stop you taking all the hope I kept inside,
You rendered me devoid then held my hand until I died.

"someone I knew and trusted tried to convince me I was insane,
and suddenly I was no longer sure what was reality and what was dream"

Rebecca Tessier, age 25
Chichester, England

in the land of immigrants

in the land of immigrants
still an immigrant.
people say to me
maybe your feeling is the feeling
of every poet
and I say
I speak and you stay silent
I cry and you laugh
I shout and you mock
I explain and you categorize
I feel pain and you run away.

"I was born in Morocco and emigrated to Israel at age 13"

Moshe Benarroch
Morocco / Israel

Lasso

I still have the old globe
the colors, the lines, the bumps -
perfectly round and tilted
as a bird might cock its head to see
a predator just a bit better.

I used to spin it, as a mother would spin
a merry-go-round, as my mother would spin
a merry-go-round with an anger that was hotter than sand.

I used to let it ride
let the pads of my fingers slide
over equator, over tropics, over topography.

The countries gliding by like paint
swatches a father would sort through,
like paint swatches my father sorted through
alone in the workshop, inhaling sawdust.

I had memorized it all, the color or things in their place.

They were married then,
shouting in the kitchen like jays, like rivers
emptying into each others wholes while
the newspapers reminded us of hostages
somewhere being held, the negotiations were breaking
down.

It was a cold war.

While I was in the den
with the globe I heard them
arguing over the way
she chopped the mushrooms
he drove at night
she didn't wear makeup
he wouldn't hug anymore

and I listened,
with the globe and the desk and the floor;
with sphere upon rectangle upon plane,
not knowing where to put it,
not knowing that the sprawling red spotch
of the Soviet Union wouldn't be there
in a couple of years,

not knowing that the patches of color
and the borders which encircled them like belts
under my fingers were
temporary.

Daniel Weinshenker
Boulder, CO, USA

SHELTERED!

What is that I hear
Falling from your lips
Words of ignorance
Expressed from a shallow, hollow mind
I have no control of the thoughts
Possessed by you or ones like yourself
As you hide in your protective shell
Choosing to pretend that the world
Is only as you wish it to be

No drug addictions
No ruthless, thoughtless crimes
No children armed with handguns
No one would ever consider robbing you blind
Only men with women
As women belong with only men
No victims left for dead
Never crossed by a friend
No callous, cheating husbands
Only humble, faithful wives
Your children will always respect your wishes
No outlandish Village nights
No beggars on the sidewalks
Kneeling at your feet
No poverty-stricken families
Waiting for you to meet

Can you ever forgive the mirror
Which reflects the face of fear
And hides all the facts and truths
That your closed mind could never bear

"I believe that `acceptance' is what we most need in dealing with social issues"

Lisa Arnone
Moonachie, NJ, USA

They say the eyes are
the windows to your soul.
Well what happens when they're drowning in tears?
It's hard to keep a soul alive
when it's buried under fears.

Emma Anderson
Figtree, NSW, Australia

Pillowtalk

You have listed
all the qualities you believe
me to possess:
Honesty Intelligence Bravery —
I am your heroin/e; Drug and Inspiration.

Your eyes cloud.
There is an aside;
having seen/heard
pictures of my dirty child-face, my
Eastend-Welfare-Booze-reared-Sally-ann
child-face, you can't help
but see me and mine (only
on occasion, mind you)
as White Trash.

The teeth in the jaws
of my clean woman-face
grit and my eyes well.
All washing, sloughing,
articulation, matriculation
is jerked away
in one swift yank.
I mumble.
Something about leaving.
Separating.

You interject with
the drama of your suffering
should I ever disappear;
My departure would
blow a hole in your heart.
And I imagine the click
as I pull the trigger behind me—

a clean hole shot through
your breast pocket,
a thin cartridge of
sunlight
coming out your shoulder blade.

If I leave now,
I will see through
you forever.

Billie Livingston
Delta, British Columbia, Canada

To Cameroon

Look, my country
Look what they have done
To your knees they strive to bring you
Invisible whips resounding in your ears

Hear me, my country
They are afraid of your freedom
And have tried to capture your voice
But your spirit can never be their own

My beautiful country
When will they ever learn
They cannot change your soul
Though they have bruised your skin

Weep not, my country
Their eyes will never comprehend
Never hear your heart beat, so strong
Like the echoing sounds of heavy native drums

Courage now, my country
Still they know no remorse for you
Not even for the children they have stolen
And are lost, for they do not know you any longer

Fear not, my country
Your essence will never leave me
For your ancient cry always beckons
And to you, I will always return.

"a crushed spirit, a dying faith and a terrible sadness caused by a loss of identity."

Kimberly Sende
Atlanta, GA, USA

Little Salmon Poem

*In the lake, in the river
when the frosty ice breaks
two little salmons shiver
a feeling of love awakes*

Andreas Bjereke
Lund, Sweden

Schnack

Slipstrafe through pools of reality.
Concept rendered: null.
Mind streamed of inhibition.
Clear patterned thoughts erode
The conscious conscience.

Skin. Flesh. Bone.
Stripped bare to nervous co-ordination.
Brain floating in the formaldehyde of space,
Nerve endings brushing the walls of insanity.

"a journey of being pushed against the glass bubble of sanity"

Daniel Ambler
South Africa

Fades to Black

You look into my eyes,
But no traces you will see,
Of what is raging inside,
Consuming the life of me.

Trying to keep it together,
Ah! I'm doing so well.
Just smile and look pretty,
See! No one can tell.

Then the waves get stronger,
Making it hard to hold in.
I was getting use to the color,
As it all fades to black again.....

"just when you feel you have it all figured out, changes come again."

exie nicks
Nashville, AR, USA

Ice-Age

Darkness surrounds me
Like a cocoon.
I don't know
Where my way leads to,
I don't know
Where I am.
I'm feeling a numbness inside.
A numbness,
that cannot even be defeated by fear.
The cold,
is crawling up,
forcing itself into each pore of my body.
It's eating through my veins
Into the depth of my soul.
The ice-age has started
And all of a sudden I know
That in my soul
There will never bloom flowers again.

Marietta Kirchen
Kaiserslautern, Germany

Sharing

×	Everybody craves multiplication;
÷	Few care about division.
$	The former creates wealth;
Δ	The latter brings justice.
+	Add your wills,
-	Subtract your suspicions,
∞	And let [the sum of] peace dawn upon you.

Ilias Chrissochoidis
Stanford, CA, USA

Anguish

My never ending journey
To the long-awaited sun,
And with promises that linger,
is the reason I wish to be done.

I'm lost in total consciousness
And deprived of Another chance.
I was taken away from everything
And left here to deny my past.

Now stranded in my solitude
And devoured by my confusion,
I am running away from an angered soul,
Which has taken my only conclusion.

Now dazed into corners of my fear
And left tortured by my sorrow,
And being ridiculed for my stands
Takes away all hopes of tomorrow.

So now I sit here all alone
And tired with a weary mind,
Not knowing what next to do
There's nothing left to find.

So I will stop this journey
To the long-awaited sun
To rest my weary Mind.
For my anguish has just begun.

But, when I continue
You'll see me cry no more
"cause my revenge is strong
And eventually...
will even the score !!!"

"sometime life can be so harsh and cruel...
one forgets what they can do to fix it"

Walking Eagle - Mike A. Sims
Santa Maria, CA, USA

Being German
(transl. I. Diggance)

Fair weather-coloured platitudes
Or simply mindless babble

It's as if one
Is choking on moon dust

And doing oneself a favour
By simply looking away

Grim
Emotionless
unfai**R**
phleg**M**atic
And
ass-licki**N**g

Sometimes
It is a merciless disgrace

To be German

And to watch
In the false company of amputated feelings

No scaffold
Separates us from the past

And the self-inflicted castration
Of an uncomfortable nature
Only brings forth
The poison-laden creature

Peter Staaden
Wiesbaden, Germany

Christiansanity

With a gun in my hand I'm a hero
With a bullet through my brain, a zero
Dead but yet so infamous
As the chanting for the imminent is so ever-present
And deafening in my ears as it rings in my head.
Kill yourself we don't care, is what it says.
The crowds and vestibules and flocks as they gather
Singing praises to the dead
Because they matter
If you are alive you cannot be a saint, be right or be good
Dead you receive all the praise and respect whether or not you should.
So the approaching scourge of mindbomb purists and martyrs
Suicide is the only way, they say, to bring you eternal life
You cannot be a man in this world unless you are dead
And everyone prays at your gravestone
And casts the honor into the blackbox, as the living are disdained.
But the dead only quickly decay into fodder and sand
No matter how much worth is pretend to be held in one hand
There is no up or down below, the casket only rots -
until it is hollow.
As I cut a bloody X into my wrists
It is what you want as your fulfillment
Of your greed for penitence, each unforgiven sin
Each word and thought and tiny beat of heart
Is a transgression which should be punished
Because the dead speak and they say, force your neighbor
To hate and slice an incision into the back of your neck
So you can remember to speak like a sheep.
And tears of sadness are the only happiness to endeavor
And still the living die and the dead rise never
Just stuck in the quicksand and not coming out
But praying to the dead
Is what is in the masses' head
And is what this misled, mixed-up, hoaxed-up world is all about.

"an atheist living under the christian `fist'…
inflicted against the will of `I-ness'…
living in a world that frowns upon open expression of the human ego"

T. S. Hunter
Glendora, CA, USA

Regret

Up the walls it climbs
tangled,
it hangs from the eves
and drapes down,
where the lilies are.
Beautiful colours swim
through our eyes
and yet we do not notice.

Unspoken words dangle
over our heads.
As we stand in trustless silence.
The reasons, the words
they all elude me now.
My senses sting
with broken promises,
and scattered dreams.

Amanda Closson
Canada

The FooLpoeM

I might be colorful
and I might paint the air
with mystical words.
I might get you to smile
from the bottom of your heart.
I might fall in love
with everything I lay my eyes upon
simply because my love
has no tags
it just is.

I might dance in the shadow of knowing
I might dance until I drop
but you see I am the fool of fools
as old as the soil
as young as the unborn
never seeking
just being
until I am no more

only my humble shadows
that I have created
to tail me into infinity.

Birgitta Jonsdottir
Reykjavik, Iceland

Wasted

I have been bound by circumstance
And bothered by your convenience
Like a child, I'm pampered by your shelter
Spoon fed and washed, everything in my desire
Listening, I can do fine, but conveying I ramble
I'm very scared inside and look I can't even tremble
I'm useless without a doubt
I'm good as a paperweight for your tabletop
For my battles you've fought and my demons you've driven
I'm eternally grateful and sorry for the inconvenience
You walk, run and talk with the greatest of ease
I hate you and the memories I cannot miss

"the resentment of one paralyzed"
Nik Tan, age 24
Republic of Singapore

A Christmas Note

If you find yourself feeling alone this season
then don't, because there's really no reason
to sit around feeling sad and blue
someone, somewhere is thinking of you.
They may not write, they may not call
they may not acknowledge that fact at all
but consider these things I say to be true
In someone's heart lies a warm place for you.

Eric H. Hollaway, Sr.
St. Petersburg, FL, USA

Belfast '98

Daffodils grow in this field,
hundreds of tiny suns on
a plate of grass.

Black boots stamp out the stars.
A flood of soldiers penetrate my field;
the men are here to

stamp out each other.
This fight started when their
grandfathers were sucking pacifiers.

This is a war over religion
This is a war about politics.
This is a war about my field.

Daffodils used to mark
where the sides would split
their territory.

No more.
Both sides have decided
that these are their flowers.

Blood is what fills my field now.
The blood of both sides
is what moistens the flowers now.

Boys grow in this field.
Hate grew from this field.

Daffodils grow in this field.

"written in the Botanical Gardens at Queen's College in Belfast"
Timothy M. Stifter
Boca Raton, FL, USA

WOMAN / CHILD

I am the Woman
Ahhh...
but
Then, I
Am the child
Gentle and sweet...
Alluring and wild
I am the match
I am the fire
The passion that burns
Enticing desire...
I am the sunshine
The
River...the rain
The scent
of sweet flowers
the dew
on your Pane
I am the woman
So strong
And so mild...
Rock me
sweet darling...
But
Cradle...the child

"I am strong...
yet with the tenderness and sensitivity of a child within me"

Theresa Bailey Delashmit
Union, MO, USA

LET ME LOVE YOU FROM A DISTANCE

HERE IN THE CATHEDRAL OF DEATH
HALF-REMEMBERED DREAMS
MAKE ME LAUGH
COME AND STEP INTO MY NIGHTMARE
JUST FOR THE SAKE OF YOUR REPUTATION
LET ME LOVE YOU FROM A DISTANCE
SO THERE IS NO PASSION LEFT
NOTHING LEFT FOR YOU TO KILL
I KNOW THE WORLD IS ONLY A DREAM
I KNOW YOUR LOVE IS ONLY A DREAM
COME AND STEP INTO MY NIGHTMARE
AND LET ME LOVE YOU FROM A DISTANCE

Sara Billingsley
San Antonio, TX, USA

Walls of Suffocation

round and round we spin
torn between right and wrong;
between right and what we want
restricted by our fears
and bound by our values
we are trapped by the walls
that we ourselves erected

Tina Ruff
Stickney, New Brunswick, Canada

When I die

What will happen to me
When I die?

Will I still yearn for the life I had thrown
For the pieces of knowledge that I'd never known
For the plentiful things that I never did
For a chance to solve all the problems I hid
from myself?

Will I weep for the people with whom I never talked
For the path of ambitions that I never walked
For a chance to be what I wanted to be
For a chance to see what I never did see
for myself?

Will I long for the happiness I never knew
If I had only achieved what I wished to pursue
For my dreams that one day I swore to fulfill
But once I am dead, I know I never will
dream again.

Will I be content as I gaze down from heaven
Or be filled with regret as I stare up from hell
For I never did live how I wanted to live
And the moment I set foot in the grave I know very well
that all my chances are gone

and I shall weep
by myself.

Aimee Rusli
Johor Bahru, Malaysia

Death

I look into her eyes, they are so deep and clear.
I feel her arms , so lean and gentle.
Her breath flows into my ears.
I hear her voice.
Sweetly and kindly she whispers promises to me.
She will keep them.
She speaks of forever, a life together, and is not afraid.
I take her hand and I feel a breath leave my lips,
I speak her name... Death.

"often our society interprets Death as an untimely executioner...
for many, though, she is an angel of mercy and compassion"

R. Keith Leach
Dover, NH, USA

Days of Unemployment and Attachment Problems

I'm the rhombus My faith in sanity is faltering as carloads of slow
deaths in swerving screams supersaturate my mind like foggy fever
hallucinations It's all in a relentlessly pounding triplicate like us
or passionless sex I stumble stagger in my muddied white
sneakers The pair's disintegrating into unstitched rubbery oblivion
Soon only ten-toed impressions encrusted into a racket of pasts that
curtly refuses to ever shut-up Swiveling on my grassy knoll, precarious
yet picturesque perch, biding time for our feline hope
to surface higher A kitten's chances old-fashioned fancies like
innocence squandered or a child cut in half in divorce There's
persistence though, like my disheveled dyed locks that sprout, yielding
not even to my scalp's infertile demands And Wza's the right angle in
our triangle
"I don't breathe where I eat," Elise boasts. "It's an idea that I've
lived my entire life around." She also claims my left ear smells like
sex, believes there's a button rotting in it
I realize the firmness of her creed and yearn
to feel the sense of confidence it's provided her with
I contemplated a friend's theory I'd heard
earlier that day; relationships are like governments and burgeon
through a system of checks and balances, she nags him about smoking too
many cigarettes and says it's a respect thing
He tries to keep her clear of the dangers of fraternity
parties, says it's a loyalty thing He cheated on her a couple
of weeks ago They click
Elise explains how strange and unstable my friendship with Wza really
is; I yell and verbally abuse him and he takes it cause he knows I need
to do it I'm only really happy
when I'm mean
I'm addicted to the milky aroma of her
exhalations It smells like chewing Twizzlers and cows
eating grass With the cows it's more the image that
reminds me, the milk process
Bill told me that the sense of smell is the one that most triggers
memories She told me that cum should be green and smells
like cows eating grass She further claims that her farts don't smell,
that she never burps and that cheap bubble bath makes her vagina
uncomfortable   Wza speculates that God must only have one
arm We named my latex severed arm Ricky; it's a righty

The three of us are writing a toilet book, a "potty book of random
thoughts" We've grown so close, knowing the comfort of being on
the same pooping schedule of someone else Elise, of course
"Today, Buddy-day, we should both be girls. I'm scared of any men
in the relationship, even if they're
me." I confessed   Her comfort lies in me rubbing her belly
while giving it a very concerned
look Wza likes to say "respiritory system" like the Scottish clone
specialist misspoke during his lecture We also liked his rich
accent Elise denied me "you no suck until you brush" my mouth green
from Blue Rasberry
Fun Dip She wants to name our cat Fun Dip We don't have her yet
but Elise still writes letters to her The other night her mouth was
green from a magic marker moustache
I didn't like it "I get to stay in the bathroom if I want. I get to do
whatever I want. I get spoiled," she incessantly boasts
I interviewed for a job to assist retarded people
"Do you have a problem washing retarded women?" the interviewer asked me
Dispensing with ideals like pride and dignity
I said "No."
I was denied the job anyway. "They tend to get very attached to our
workers and since you're only going to be here until the summer, I think
it would be better if I just hired another candidate. However, if you
were interested in working as a volunteer...?"
I'm poor, but I'll wash no one's crotch for free. I wish I was spoiled.
Shathex or Bowerex-partaking in a shared bath, a shower, and then sexual
relations, respectively
Wza has been forced into the role of the right angle in the triangle
The three of us claim to be specific geometric shapes, or maybe
only I do Our kitchen's so small
the refrigerator is in the living
room

We arose to a dawn truly chilling and our car tires
popped on the vet's curb
We ignored the bad omens
and took the kitten anyways

*"struggling to make sense of ourselves and this world,
where the sense behind everything is always in question"*

Jon Petruschke
Fort Washington, PA, USA

"Another Good Time"

Clouded eyes,
Dripping throat,
Smoked filled lungs.
Pixies dance on the rug of my brain.
Twisted thoughts,
of Passion and Wisdom.
Tripping down a dreamscape
with the grace of a clown.
Clock strikes 3.
The night falls upon my shoulders,
like an over bearing cross.
Eyes like the horizon at sunset.
Worn face,
Tattered soul.
I'd like to lie down
and sleep for eternity.

Jim Healey, age 26
Cleveland, OH, USA

INTO THE GARDEN

I WALK DOWN THE DARKENED STREET
TO A PLACE I HAD FORGOTTEN
THROUGH THE GATE
INTO THE GARDEN
WHERE LOVE ONCE FLOURISHED
AND CHILDREN ONCE PLAYED
WHERE LAUGHTER WAS HEARD
AND TEARS WERE BRUSHED AWAY

I SAT AMONGST THE LILACS
THEIR AROMA SO DIVINE
AND LINGERING IN THEIR SCENT
WERE WELCOMED MEMORIES
OF CHILDHOOD GAMES
AND ROMANTIC NIGHTS
WHEN LAUGHTER WAS HEARD
AND TEARS WERE BRUSHED AWAY

AND IN THE MIDST OF LIFE
I FOUND MYSELF REFLECTING
ON SIMPLE THINGS
FROM SIMPLE TIMES
OF A LIFE THAT GREW
AND WAS THROWN AWAY
WHEN LAUGHTER WAS SELDOM HEARD
AND TEARS FLOWED EVERY DAY.

Judy Gripton
Iowa, USA

THE DIALECTICIAN

I AM CHRYSOSTOM.
I DON'T EXPECT YOU TO UNDERSTAND.
I STAND AT THE PREACHER'S PULPIT
AND PROJECT AN ENDLESS ARRAY OF WORDS

AND ENCHANT YOU -
WITH ABSTRACTIONS.

AND YOU PRETEND THAT YOU UNDERSTAND,
AND I PRETEND THAT I AM AS DEEP AS
PERDITION, WHERE ATLANTIS SLEEPS,
BURIED IN A PLATONIC DREAM.

THE MOON IN TARSUS, MOVED
AND I IN TARTARUS, DOOMED

TO ASSUME THE PROPHET'S ROLE,
A NOSTRADAMUS FORECASTING
STORMY WEATHER IN QUATRAINS
HIDDEN FROM ACADEMIC WITCH HUNTERS.

I SPEAK OF PLACES AND PEOPLE
AND THINGS -

THINGS IN METAPHORS -
AND THINGS THAT ALLUDE
TO OTHER THINGS. ALL THE WHILE,
YOU SIT IN CAPTIVE DELIGHT
AND CONTEMPLATE MEANING.

PAST, PRESENT, AND FUTURE,
FRAMED IN EINSTEIN'S SINISTER MIND.

I CONVERSE WITH DEAD POETS
WHO RISE FROM EARTHEN TOMBS,
DECLARING THEIR TRICKERY
THROUGH THE WITCH OF ENDOR - IN ABSTRACTIONS, OF COURSE.

MIMICKING POUND,
LOSING MYTH IN REALITY.

YOU WANT TO KNOW?
EVEN MY OWN LIPS RECOIL
WHEN I CONSIDER THE END OF ALL THINGS.
SHOULD I TELL YOU THE TRUTH?

"as the millennium approaches, we witness an increasing number of prophets forecasting doom and despair"

Frank S. Palmisano III
Baltimore, MD, USA

The Return.

She is closed now,
The asylum.
Blinded with boarding
Hiding her shame.

How sad to see the gardens shabby,
The paint work shoddy,
The canteen sour with stale food,
The walkways dirty.

Down the corridors running through time
The staff rooms,
The time out rooms,
The day rooms, where parents would pretend to care
While their offspring just rocked and stirred.
All deserted now - smoking with ghosts.
A tear in my eye.

Like fountains belching bile the tin Gods that ruled,
With fists of steel, spouted fourth.
Their long sins gone,
Their promises turned to dust.

The subways are catacombs of crumbling tunnels,
Where only rats can run.
And the tormented souls of the undead roam.

She is closed now,
The asylum.
I am free of her.
But the silent screams of the sightless
Disfigured damaged children,
Will haunt me to my grave.

"a return visit to a closed asylum where I worked for many years"
Roy Shepherd
Darwen, Lanc, England

This Thing Called Rap

Just what is this thing called rap
To most adults it sounds like crap
Violence, drugs, sex, and death
It makes them gasp and hold their breath
But is something deeper in these songs
Try listening to see what's going on
The age we live in is really trying
A lot of people are sick and dying
Most rap reflects reality
Just like a news show on T.V.
Though all the lyrics aren't real
Many let us know the real deal
Aren't all the elements of these songs
A part of our world's going ons
I think they are I surely do
Just read the paper and you will too
A bad influence, not to me
Still some will say it could be
But they say the same about T.V.
So before you go and plug your ears
Listen to their hopes, dreams, and fears
You just might understand today's youth
And realize that it's not so uncouth
For Easy, Pac, and Biggie Smalls
All wrote poetry, one and all.

J C
Columbia, MO, USA

Homophobe

Oh I swallow gay literature
Like a catacomb holding bodies
'Til it overflows.
To see how our loves and lives
Lasted the centuries.
Your hate rising and falling
With each decade,
Not lasting for nought but your
Tiny lifetime.
Our words ring our freedom
And our persecution
For the ends of time to hear.
With words and paintings
And people holdings placards
Being photographed.
Our images flood the mass unconscious
Saying 'Love is not a gender.'

I see you rise.
I see you fall.
I see you.
I see you.

I see your children.

Your children learning
All your spitting-spike lies.
About sodomic-hell
And blowjob-purgatory for eternity.
Children talking to faeries in their gardens
Wondering why fairies shall become a slash at someones throat.
I look at innocence being tainted
And that one that happens to be
Like the ones you despise, shoots himself.
Bang!

Will you only learn then?
Will you only understand where your lies
Run like bullets into your son's heads.
Not only your sons but your daughters, sisters, brothers, uncles
            and aunts; grannies and grandfathers;
            and that man you saw walking along the street
With sadness in his eyes
Because he liked the slope of your chest
Leading down.

I get angry most times
But its cools off
And I remember where I come from:
Love.
I remember when you and I mixed in essence together
And decided to play this part down here on Gaia.
So I try to live the love I am inside
Where God lives easy under dirt.

A hug before I depart
And leave these words to ponder in your heart,
Remember where we came from
For there is no you and I.
Remember how your children came into this world
without a prejudice to think about.
Remember love oh please remember love
Because I take my scars from you
And leave quietly,
But I'd rather share my light with you.
Thank you for your ears and attention
So I leave now.
May these words bare heavy on your heart.

Ivo Visic, age 17
Johannesburg, South Africa

Of One House

With Steely Nerved Ignorance
Swooning Waves Roll Over
Tiny Pawns
Leaving Behind Crumpled Remains
Of Their Own Flesh and Blood
Struggling With That Which
Feeds Their Veins
Burning the Beds
On Which They Sleep
Breaking Brothers' Truths
And Telling Promises
They Can't Keep

*"from watching the news and seeing disturbing images of wars...
waged for reasons that are hard to comprehend...
against our own family, the human family"*

Ben Brant
Rostock, Ontario, Canada

Thanksgiving Prayer

Thank you for letting my ancestors
Rape and pillage this land.

Thank you for making the natives so naive
And letting us slaughter them all.

Thank you for creating slaves
To prepare the bounteous harvest.

Thank you for the machines
That demolish and kill so efficiently.

Thank you for the plagues
That kill off "undesirables".

Thank you for giving parents
Freedom from responsibility and blame.

Thank you for the knowledge
That we really are better than them.

Thank you for widespread ignorance
So the poor don't rise up in revolution.

Thank you for the taboos
That keep incest and abuse private.

Thank you for justice
To protect those who can afford it.

Thank you for the democracy
That let's us blame the other guy.

Ms. Cydniey
West Chester, PA, USA

"Reflections on 11/14/97"

Smooth,
cool to the touch.
Can you see your image?
Waiting for diamond words
while you look through me.
Empty rooms
with hard chairs.
You're uninvited
so sit down,
make yourself uncomfortable,
and put your fist
through my pane.

"I had just tried to leave my husband...again...unsuccessfully"

Danna Jae Botwick
Las Vegas, NV, USA

a chance encounter with relish

rubbed on my spice! shadows stolen! scorpions!
witchcraft! EGGPLANTS! conspiratorial
democracies! witnessing victims! contemplative
seizures!
drumming a rhythm on the skin
the angel sings
with the headlines speaking of lukewarm obviousies
i turned to taste the light spinning in a miracle of
spiderwebbing glass and waterlilies the cello
moaned my heart kept thumping weaker and
stronger steam rose from a hole in the dirt a rabbit
bounced away the vision came to me in the
morning speaking of syncristic crystalline in the
metaphysical presence of the thick vermilion night
i fell away piece by piece electric and quite blue
myself DRUNK AGAIN after fourteen years of
celibacy I got screwed
on whiskey!! it felt goooood like candles...
burning...or the sweet taste of candy she said she
didn't know that history repeated itself and it was i
that left earlier than she thought it was the whiskey
all along and the tenderness she crept into my
wildhorse dreams of shaking fetlocks and high with
stallion craziness i ordered one more it was the
end of my life as far as I was concerned
trivial and all too real

"I had broken up with my girlfriend, everything seemed to be coming apart. I went with a
friend for a drink, not the norm for me, where I got talking with a woman,
until her ex-boyfriend showed and whisked her away"

Michael J. Nedell
Burlington, VT, USA

The answer

I thought you were the answer.
The only answer.

I had obviously
misunderstood
the question.

Cathrine Lødøen
Oslo, Norway

Anguish is my only Friend

Anguish is my only friend, always standing by my side.
Night's my sister, Blood's my dad, and Darkness is my Bride.

My soul consists of flames, burning from my heart.
The darkness burns inside me, and that is just the start.

The winds of change are blowing, they blow right at my face,
But I turn away and wither, refuse to run this race.

The world revolves before me, I stand beyond and look.
Blood that covers both my hands, reminds me what I took.

Have you ever looked Death in the Eyes?
It's a cold gaze staring back.
Have you ever heard her laughter?
It is Evil, it is Black.

I consume all darkness, I absorb all light.
The only thing shining, is my hatred so bright!
I am what is dark, and I fear what is true.
The thing most denied, is my love for you.

My life is sad and lonely, my days and nights - dead ends!
The Darkness and the Anguish, are indeed my only friends.

Magnus Johnson
Sôderhamn, Sweden

ABUSE

She screams inside herself,
words too hot to be spoken freely.
Words heard often by the dog
that sometimes comes around.

She suffers the common-ground of indecency,
felt much to often by her kind.
Batterment by large bones,
against smaller bones.
Batterment felt often by the dog
that sometimes comes around.

A single drop of blood.
A morning rose that stains her pillow.
Last night's disappointment she recalls;
A beating while cowering against a wall.
Beatings given often by the dog
that sometimes comes around.

Ernest Serna, a.k.a. "Goat"
Laurel, MD, USA

HOLD ONTO HOPE

Hold onto hope
That wants to slip through
Keep dreaming your dreams
For they make everything new
The weak and weary will stand
On hope they continue to hold
When the wild wind blows
They will never feel the cold

Hold onto hope
As echoes light the flame
Change the pace in things you do
So that nothing seems the same
Bring back the desire of yesterday
While children laugh in delight
Delegate your memories told
So everything stays in the light

Hold onto hope
While your heart swells within
Accept what you know can change
As any virgin can sin
Remember darkness sees no color
Because it has no eyes
But now it's time to take notice
Of every single thing that cries

Hold onto hope
For silence asks you to follow
Now you feel clouds strain
As you try to eat your pride and swallow
Now forces of the past refrain
From telling you how to live life
Take a hand in each and squeeze
Because alone we are left in strife

Hold onto hope
So we can take in the scenery
Seasons change often
Which keeps hope for spring's greenery
All the while, the rich get richer
While the poor keep dreams to confess
So tell the old man he can smile
Because money doesn't equal happiness

Now the glory can finally be told
The needs of humanity will grow
But if you suppress all your hopes
Then no one will ever know
In time, all things will settle into place
We'll have the answers as to how to cope
But we will never know what we can achieve
If we don't hold onto hope

Christopher Stolle
Richmond, IN, USA

Loneliness is love

From a fragrant
hollow of the night
the braying of a tick
tock care:

You
not more than a pigeon
an ordinary bird
among thousands all sitting
high atop some Venetian Cathedral

Nearby gondolas murmur in
forgotten tongues
the long dark poles push
in the water, releasing
reflections
of moonlight
like a flood of whispers

To you
I hold out my hand
filled with crumbs, and
as your bony feet dig
into my skin
I know
I will never be
more lonely.

*"one can travel a long distance to achieve a feeling,
then without warning another intrudes...
the impact and proximity of each is then revealed"*

Eldad Malamuth
Seattle, WA, USA

"'cause i still do feel so horribly lonely"
- s.morrissey, from his song "Ouija Board"

I need another drink
even one more
sadness hit me in a bad way
i just have myself
it's never enough,
only white sheets to fill
a cup of coffee looks at me
tears running away forever
night rots me
i've said it so many times
but now is different
i've found another hue on it
songs end, minutes flow
and i still feel so horribly lonely

Alvaro r. Lopez
Antofagasta, Chile

I Only Want a Taste

Please don't make me guess
I don't want to have to consider
the implications
of your expression.
Please don't spell it out for me
I don't want to have to realize
I don't want to recognize
this moment: Almost passionate
                Bursting toward compassionate
We could be teetering past friendship,
But that is sure to make me fall.
I only want a taste
like
the scent of cotton candy
without the sticky mess.

Please
Whitewash your emotion
Paint your sex in pastel colors
It might be nice
to feel you come
but do not make me cross that bridge myself.
If I taste you now
will I tap you and wrap you for the rest of my life?
I cannot recover from an addiction of that magnitude.
And yet
Perhaps
You could finally sate my hunger
But what if you did?
When one ceases to be hungry, what can one do
but sleep?

Actually
I'm afraid of satisfaction
I know that it cannot be obtained
In the end
I'm avoiding completion
I don't know what to do when the act is done.

Jonathan Penton
Marietta, GA, USA

Café Rebellion

Oh you're a rebel -
your haircut proves it
and your friends love
your careful cafe politics
and revolutionary chic

how radical your clothes are
and your brand of cigarettes,
your way of dress and speaking
could trigger great events
to be remembered

you're a fashion fascist
a narrow-minded nabob
of nihilism, postmodern style,
first among your unequals
black your favourite colour

in clothing that is
not the flag of anarchy
or the pigmented people
proud they're not you,
comfortable and relaxed

your mind untormented
searches for a remark
fit for a rebel, without
a cause, that's too uncool
for someone like you

all those who really care
they're just not in style,
its not hip to criticise
without coffee in hand,
fingers firmly crossed

so go on critiquing
the latest band you hate
writer who's a fake
and while your wanking
I'll put my uncool shoulder to the wheel

"revolutionary chic is in,
but how many actually challenge the status quo?"

Darren Jones
Clarence Park, South Australia

Land of The

I am the crack baby
Hooked before birth
Doomed to tread this earth
Restless, violent, hopeless
But that's O.K. . . .
I am the AIDS victim
My body a concentration camp
And I its soul inmate
Praying for a cure, waiting for death
But that's O.K. . . .
I am the welfare mother
No job, no money, no future
Will you stop that crying
Oh baby I'm sorry, mommy doesn't mean to hurt
But that's O.K. . . .
I am the bigot
And no left wing, nigger-loving
Half-kike—half-mick bastard
Is gonna put me in no pansy ass poem
But that's O.K. . . . . This is America

Craig Bertuglia
Hattiesburg, MS, USA

Scarecrow

The scarecrow stands all alone in the desert of my heart,
like Christ crucified upon the cross.
The wheat field as gold as the desert beneath him,
and just as barren.
He stands alone,
yet full of purpose,
an apathetic state with no heart.
His facade scares off all antipathy.
The crops of love ripe
and ready for the picking,
protected from the black vultures of hate.

"about innocence...
an adverse facade put on by those truly lonely at heart"

Chris Jones
Kambah, ACT, Australia

SHOTS OF YELLOW

INDUSTRIAL CHILDREN DEATH!
HIDDEN ADDRESS OF THE EYES!
SHOTS FROM THE BRAIN!
HITLER INSANE!
PRACTICAL DEATH INSIDE OF THEIR DREAMS!
SEW MY EYES SHUT WITH HUMAN HAIR!
THE HORNS BLARE!
THE SOUND OF BOMBS WHISTLE FROM THE AIR!
POLITICAL SEATS UNWED!
IDOLS NOW FED!
LET THE HUNGER BEGIN!
MARXIST INSANE!
ARMOR MINDS!
TWISTED CRIMES!
BABIES DISEMBOWELED!
BLOOD FORMS THE GROUND!
IS MAN INSANE

OR IS IT JUST US?

"how the 20th century has affected our generation's politics of thought"

Cam Rea, age 21
Kendallville, IN, USA

In Reference to Susan, an Apple Halved and Browning

"Now that I have watched you eat an apple
my hand is lonely unless an apple fills it."
Susan Mitchell, from "For a Friend Eating an Apple"

Think of Susan when you look at me;
that ripe taste of autumn
and the feel of burlap against your skin.
I know how it feels to be an apple,
pressed against the flat ecru of your teeth:
the anticipation
of that first spurting bite.
There is something natural about this exchange
that summons childhood reverence.
I see us together
in a sea of bright Irish green,
though I know you grew up in Buffalo, and I
somewhere east of Asheville. When was it
that we found ourselves? Was it the summer
we caught fireflies on that rolling soccer field?
The grass there was slick and dark,
and we both wore a little of it back to our rooms
after saying goodnight.
I can remember the lawnmower smell
brushed off the backs of our legs,
and how it mingled with the incense I burned
later that evening. I showered,
but I could still feel the summer-struck wind
that leapt from your hand to mine.
How many times did we roll down that hill?
It felt new and wet every time,
and I lost all sense of numbers.
You say you kept time in your head,
and I know musicians sometimes do.
At night, I imagine us against that mass of earth,
and that it's your silhouette I see
from the laundry room's third story window. Tomorrow
I'll want to whisper the word "sunset" in your ear,
but I'll find there is some other tune for you to follow.
We'll take a little time to walk then,
and you'll fail to notice somebody's lost apple,
halved and browning, in the grass.

"Too often it isn't mutual affection that drives the heart
but individual infatuation...
a shame we can't survive on imaginative speculation"

Katherine LaLima
Summerville, SC, USA

THOUGHTS ON NOISES

It's kinda a weird night
Maybe 'cause I'm all alone
And I think the tap's drippin' again
Better let Daddy fix it
After all, he's the boss
Ain't he?
I suppose it's going to be one of those fret filled nights
When tension builds
Until someone falls off the ladder
Kinda sad
I guess we're what Mr. Lennon
Would call Working Class Heroes
Or something of the sort
It's nice to be called something
Besides girl and kid
There's that bloody noise again
Could be rats
But then, there ain't no rats in our beautiful country
At least, from what they let you see
I don't doubt that somewhere downtown
A kid my age
Hears real rats
But that's the least of her worries
Naw, we don't hear about that
We give money to charities
Feel good about ourselves
Never hear about it again
There are many ways to be blind
And it ain't hard
To plug your ears, either
In fact, if you wanted to
You could build a wall around yourself
Call it success
or popularity
I'd rather see the horizon
And hear the bloody gore of life
If you don't mind, Mr.
So what do you think of God, sir
Oh sorry, too personal
I'll say I understand
I'll say the Our Father
I'll say poor people bring it on themselves
Yes sir
Funny, he wouldn't have answered my question
Anyway
Neither would Mommy
Or the Sunday school teacher
Funny

There's that bleepin' noise
Could be a ghost
Wonder what the Sunday school teacher would say
To that
I always thought Jesus
Was a ghost at one point
He was a teenager, too
God bless that dirty word
Dirty young people with their dirty ways
'Spose Jesus wasn't a punk
But there ain't no denying he was a rebel
Just like the type that keep protesting
And the government keeps telling to shut-up
Funny
Daddy hasn't fixed the tap yet
Maybe I should

"based on emotions I felt after hearing of student protests in British Columbia, and elsewhere"

Jen Burgess, age 15
Alberta, Canada

In the Streets of the City

Footsteps thunder, people lumber,
In the streets of the city.
Chaos reigns, glamour feigns,
Inside the busy city.

Lightning flashes, she always dashes,
As she moves about the city.
Noises roar, he claims a score,
Vulgarity -- king of the city.

Smoke blows, nothing grows,
Grey and brown city.
Little health, quicksilver wealth,
Flows about the city.

Head swirls, darkness curls,
About me in the city.
Madness falls, mind in walls,
Walls me in the city.

Julia Nolan
Benicia, CA, USA

The song of a mad singer

*...so, you've closed your eyelids
forever...taking away the breath
from my songs and filling the lungs
of death with it all...
As if you had had enough of
charming the earth with your
eyes, ears, hands and feet...
you've moved over to heaven
to continue enchanting...
The whispers you poured
into the lonely moon...
the breath you infused the
orphaned flowers with...
the anklets you've
changed dewdrops into...
the music your light touches
brought out from the dead logs...
the 'live man' that you
transformed this dead being into
....
all these now, all these now
are lying bereft of the
essential 'YOU'...
Lying my head in the secret
lap of mysteriously sad night,
my eyes filling up with
the 'sweat of sorrow'...
I lie silently, dreaming
a dream of joining your
heavenly dreams...*

"the outpouring of a forlorn youth whose ladylove has breathed her last in her prime"

V. Mariappan
Tamil Nadu, South India

observation

I sit, wondering
as the rain comes to the lake
why it jumps for joy
as bullets of rain crash down
on its now broken surface

*"the special serene place we all have in our hearts
...where we go to reflect"*

Ben Brant
Rostock, Ontario, Canada

Bastard Quicktime Movies

Reading like late period
Scorcese movies in a shotglass prism,
with a maraschino blaxsploitation
Jefferson's feel - Jackie Wilson over an
anti-gothic Brooklyn - a nakedness, brutal
and harshly stimulating; a club at closing time
with the lights on, nothing to do but move on;
a kick in the ass
that momentarily sets one frozen
cools the burning
from beneath the eyes;
on those indescribable days when neither sun nor
scent prods him or strips away the mucus-like patina
of depression's fatigue, he is powered,
infused at times by a blended
whisky of a secret mixture.
Distilled, coded, embedded,
condensed, ancient memories
mixed with many different,
specific, topical ingredients.
He hated the fact
that he loved to hate loving them.
A giant funhouse exposed to daylight -
the spooky characters of each petrified vignette
animated by a milquetoast, Rockwell
chiaroscuro.
A recipe kaleidoscopic -
Ever-changing subliminal get well cue cards on flash paper -
Fleeting and Pure-
Tangible Curiosity of sunny day formaldehyde freedoms
dancing vibrantly like a bug in amber on the corners
of Flatbush and Nostrand -
A cerebral dressing, meshing peppered roofs atop compacted
Tudor style mysteries into
the power of the Philip Howard
and down the Orange Julius sluice
before it can separate,
a sly, imaginative virtual nostalgia of idealization
so potent it stops him dead
in the process of making his strong coffee -
Spring trees, half-naked, whisk creativity, confusion
and anger into the cerulean blue
expanse of analog daydreams above Mansfield Gardens-
A morosely beautiful, noxious, jarring elixir -
A fragrant smelling salt vision strong enough
to make a strip mall wilt and die -
disappearing at a pace swifter than a
split second improvisation
on a theme unrecorded.

*"Standing by the sink as WBGO broadcasts its glorious `Rhythm Review'
with Felix Hernandez"*

Sunshine
Freehold, NJ, USA

LIGHT AND DARK

IN THE SHADOWS OF MY MIND
SOLEMN SPECTERS MURMUR ARCHITECTURAL DARKNESS
ETHEREAL LANDSCAPES OUT FROM LIPS OF CLAY

IN THE DREAMSCAPE OF MY LIFE
BLAZING CACOPHONY, FAMILY AND FRIENDS
CRY OUT TO ME: "THE SUN IS FLYING AWAY!"

IN MY INNER SANCTUARY, DARK YET COMFORTING
A PHANTASMAGORICAL CONTRAST TO THE GARISHNESS OF THIS EXISTENCE
YET STILL IMPERFECT; FOR SILENCE IS CLOSER TO PEACE THAN POEMS

IN MY LIFE: THE GARISH COLORS HURT MY EYES
IN MY MIND: THE BLACK I KNOW SO WELL
WHETHER TO BE BLINDED BY THE LIGHT OR ENVELOPED INSIDE:
WHICH IS THE WORSE? WHO CAN TELL?

Elizabeth A.B. Hughes, age 17
Black Eagle, MT, USA

Surrounded by friends, she thinks
no one can hurt me now
not considering the fact that
she sleeps alone
Darkness points out details and
stars shine on razorblades, while
the moon preoccupies the mind
She doesn't cry - never will, but
thoughts come and go at a rapid pace
In the morning they vanish, but
they have left their mark
she pulls on a long-sleeved shirt,
along with a smile

Jennifer Lynn Pinder
Cobleskill, NY, USA

Drop Dead

Shall I or shall I not?

Simple to disappear, to disintegrate, to fragment
The scarlet veins open to falacies
Like the vampire of wrists ripped
To empty my tormented, infected soul
World stand darkened, cancelled
Knives razored on smeared floors
Bathwater painted sweet Russian
Reflections of tears raced mascara
Ribbons of sadness stream
Tighten bows twisting hedges
Swallow me for Lucifer's fires
For tempted bottled concoctions vertigo
Addicted to fantasised fate
To devilled, cooked death
Incinerate the empty false voices
Grilled, sweltering for pointless sexed days
Humming like the warrior bees
Bullet speed temple rage
Drips of red fashioned my face
Phone sings dialtone blank
Friends sweat dire superficiality
Spy at the nylon weaved tights
To braid around the neck in cobra's poison
To suffocate, sublimate, suppurate
Like the cyanosed children of the obscure Jude
Stopped, ceased, emptied, gone.

Shall I or shall I not?

"as a doctor, I'm exposed to a widespread, widely-ignored problem in our society - the desperation of suicide"

Rita Pal
Sutton Coldfield, England

The Good Life

We keep slamming into the same old walls,
it somehow makes us feel alive. It's okay, you say,
the blood of wounds can taste more real than
day to day successes.

And if I tried to explain this to the rest of the world,
I'd be laughed back into silence by the common folk
as they wait for their fairytale dreams, three cars in the garage,
and house just like, only better than, their neighbors.

But I'm here now, among friends and understanding.
I'm embraced by the present and all it means
to not have to explain why I am here or why
it matters that I am.

Kris Schultz
Columbia, SC, USA

waiting room

i have no advice for tangled seaweed,
grab a mermaid? stick to a rock? find religion?
i don't know - but i'm dealin' with it
dealin' with seasons in hell, slippery
sporadic / regular / temporary /
like dice against table sides,
when they settle -
they settle on snake eyes,
so this is growin' up,
this is fallin' down,
this is leanin' over,
this is change for my dollar,
this is slot machine life
you can have my coin -
i'm going home,
goin' home t build card castles
and i'm not the only one
believin' there's a queen of hearts inside,
there was / she moved
the rest fell down - (it's the carpenter's fault)
but i'm tryin' - to capture that confusion
for a few - under the lights,
swimmin' through the smoke,
dealin' - one card at a time,
i remember an olds 88,
i remember rust,
grew briefly on a raised ranch,
spoke this to a girl once -
she left me for the sea,
i confronted my fish foe like captain aihab,
and let me tell you - she took my fingers,
now i'm dealin' with the waiting room,
we're all in someone's waiting room,
even if they're not human / a friend / lover / a god
so what you readin'? is it outta date?
dealin' - with a most peculiar/ particular rage -
when you come this way
squeezin' my brains dry,
spitting fury fire, flyin' eagle high,
your sandpaper, dry skin,
your harsh, hard, high heel click,
the long windin' country road
sailin' ship trip led you here(?)

feelin' speechless (?)
- not you, not eye,
me droppin' drool from i,
the ceiling sky / white,
like a flashlight teases night,
or a night tease us,
you bumble, mumble, stumble
o'er the shoes, you stumble in all day -
what brought you here?
dealin' / feelin'
like the street / concrete...
need a tick tack mint snack
to cool this heat,
i remember better times
on the ranch, on a hill, on a high
before "goodbye"
before "hi" - hello / hell - low
before the turn / the return
eyes said this burns
BUT i'm GOIN' HOME,
not gonna be stuck on you,
wearin' my own harpoon.

Kain
Amsterdam, NY, USA

THE OBJECT

SLOW HYPNOTIC MOTIONS
TURNING SHADOWS TO COLOR
IN A BLINK
COUNTLESS MASTERFUL WIRES,
ORCHESTRATING A SPIRITED DANCE
TIPPING AND BOUNCING
MIMICKING LIFE'S UNPREDICTABILITIES
WITH SUCH UNCERTAIN ACCURACY
IT'S OWN CONDENSED HARMONIOUS
UNIVERSE
REACHING OUT BEYOND ITSELF,
AND SPEAKING WITH A CHILDISH
INNOCENCE
HUMANITIES GOLDEN VOICE
A FRAGILE BALANCE, WITH
HOPE AS THE SUSTAINING THEME
A CATALYST FOR FORGING
ANY DREAM

"inspired by Alexander Calder"

Brent J. Ratkovich
Napa, CA, USA

Pleading For An Answer

I lay awake alone in bed
Conscious of the fire that touches my skin
Breathing in the stale air of my room
My eyes searching vainly for something
Something - an answer
An answer to a question I hold within me
My breath comes in uncanny slow rasps
As my skin continues to burn
Burning for his touch
My ears become sensitive to every movement
Hoping to hear an answer
To a question not yet known
Heartbeats pound loudly in my chest
Making me clearly aware of my own mortality
Limiting the time I have on earth
But still I do nothing
Seeking a free answer -
An easy way out
From laying alone in my bed

Amy Herbert, age 17
Oshawa, Ontario, Canada

Hope

Bloodshot lines run through a heroin eye,
as a bloodred sun falls from a cocaine sky.
And as the day closes and comes to an end,
his world breaks down at the loss of his only friend.
He has nowhere to run,
he has nowhere to hide,
as American culture takes a stab at his side.
Wither, blister, burn, and peel,
all that he can do is kneel.
He bows to false gods known as enjoyment,
he prays to them in lines of unemployment.
As his life slips away he plants his seeds of sorrow,
and he rises once more just to dig his own harrow.
As this husk of a man digs his own hole,
he tries one last time, and lets God save his soul.
He dies and is happy for the first time in awhile,
and rising toward heaven he finally cracks a smile.

"the grief and trials of life,
and the hope of some greater place awaiting our arrival"

Abigail Keisler, age 14
Fort Wayne, IN, USA

Day's Exit

At the end of the day,
I settle among scattered thoughts.
An autumnal burden,
that I need to shed
for a winter of carelessness.

Unfinished tasks,
uncomfortable silences,
a gathering of What Ifs,
(more than a day's worth)
crowd me,
like leaves on tired branches.

Some tremble for finality,
more than others.
An end that comes down to
settling a fear
of losing promiscuous youth
to love.

Nothing new will blossom
in this season.
The decomposed weight of years past
lies at my feet.

I want to clear it away,
or bury it with another problem
unresolved.

Though deep beneath the pile
between roots
it came together.

Somewhere in that living debris
that blew in with the twenty year storm
I saw my father leave me.

*"There is a lot going on `between roots' that is suppressed by society...
poetry is my attempt at liberation"*

Grant Spencer
Georges Hall, NSW, Australia

LIFE BUMBLES

LIFE ROLLS AND BUMBLES
AND STUMBLES AND FALLS
BETWEEN THE CRACKS
OF PURPOSE AND MEAN

AND CALLS AND CRUMBLES
AND BECKONS AND FOLDS
AND STANDS ALONE
YET ALWAYS LEANS

LOVE STAINS AND BURNS
AND CHASTISES AND BENDS
WITHIN THE FRAMES
OF REALIZE AND GIVE

AND ABSORBS AND LEARNS
AND ACHES AND TAKES
AND ASKS ONLY FOR A REASON TO LIVE.

Natasha Jones
Parsonsburg, MD, USA

Another

Another party
And I don't get invited
Another kiss
On someone else's lips
Another half-truth
And a dozen might-be's
How can I care
When care has slipped?

"regret...what if's..."

Torsten C. Kathke, age 18
Ulm, Germany

TRANSCENDING

FOREVER...WE LIVE THROUGH ETERNITY...
EACH PASSING LIFETIME
FORMS AND FLOWS INTO THE NEXT...
DO WE REALIZE THE SIGNIFICANCE OF IT ALL?

SPIRITUALLY AND EMOTIONALLY CONNECTED...
A DESTINY...FEW EXPERIENCE
SELDOM WISH TO...
OR PERHAPS FAIL TO RECOGNIZE THE CALL...

BEYOND OUR DREAMS...
OUR PHYSICAL BEINGS...
SOULS REACH OUT IN THE VOID...
HOPING TO ENDURE THE PAIN OR EXPLORE THE PLEASURE...
CONNECTED THROUGH TIME...

IS IT LOVE WE REMEMBER...
OR A STRANGENESS THAT BINDS
SO STRONG THAT NOTHING CAN FREE
OR DISILLUSION...
TRANSCENDING EVERYTHING WE UNDERSTAND...
SPINNING A TALE, A POEM, A RHYME...

REACHING OUT TO HOLD THE TRUTH
IN SUCH TINY PALMS
FEELING ONLY THE LIMITS...
THE BOUNDARIES OF LIFE...
MIRACLES APPEAR...
FOR SOMETIMES...
WE FEEL THE GREATNESS AND THE BEAUTY OF IT ALL.

*"our soul does not die but continues to live on,
as in the cycle of 9 lives,
joining kindred souls for eternity"*

Seika
Ontario, Canada

Period Piece

**As the caboose of Generation X
clatters and stumbles
its way to the Career Development Office**

**across the lawn
littered with recycled paper,
they are too conscious
of what earlier ages
had to discover:**

the past is always
hipper than the present
literary figures don't have to
eat ramen or pay ten cents a minute
the past has periods the present
has papers the future would like
fries with its order

studying sex is easier
than gettin' any
and romance was a period
from 1800-1830

your B.A. is useful
for jotting down employers'
phone numbers go
to a party or a show
and twitch,
twitch

twitch

Gary Wilkens
Conway, AR, USA

SKY GLANCING

A misunderstood and clouded sky promises intermittent thunderstorms.
Bright seasonable sunlight bursts through denying the inevitable.
The humid heat exacts precipitation in our solitary selves.
The crisp prayer-like breeze cools our taut tumultuous bodies.
Creating a misconstrued maze of uncertainty and confusion.
We walk through thoughtfully not knowing of where to step, or of how to touch.
We are not sure whether to smile at the sun, or grimace at the rain.
Completely uncertain of which is best for us.
Is it necessary to plant the seed and wait for rain?
Or let it rain then plant the seed?
A decision that must be made without the help of weather man or farmer.
A resolution only we can make.
We intently struggle with alternatives.
While uncomfortable time steals happiness.
Yet we wait, sky glancing.

"whether good friends should remain that way, or become lovers"

Gavin R. Baker
KwaZulu/Natal, South Africa

starting over is not as easy as you think,
when you start over, you might lose your link
to the precious life that was so sad
and all the choices once gone bad.
And don't forget your land's tradition,
when you start living in your new condition;
but to start over, I must guess –
we kill ourselves to become someone less.

Vladimir A. L. Tauberman, age 16
Los Angeles, CA, USA

LUST

I loaned my jumper

> *now its soft scent describes you.*

You hauled it on
trowel smoothed its shape
arranged
> *neck band*
>> *cuffs*
>>> *hem   as a... soldier adjusts sights.*

>>> *Inside*
>>> *I*
>>>> *slid*
>>> *egg yoke runny*
>>>> *away.*

Later
my gift lay... discarded on a chair.
I filled myself
with your fragrance
greedy for any remnant.

Now I lie
beanbag marooned
curled round thoughts... taboo images.

My mind holds the power
to stall this... foetal course, this...
marsupial progress.

But not the will.

Not
the will.

Tania Lawrence
Victoria, Australia

Longing

Looking back on my life
I remember a time
Carefree and pure and nothing unsure.
Here I am now
Longing for it all to come back
Wondering where along the lines I lost track.
Longing for the beauty, the simplicity,
The innocence of a child.
If only I could
Go back a few years
Be back in a time
Where I had no fears
Back where there existed no tears
No worries, no pain
But my longing's in vain.
I can only move towards the future
Uncertain, unstable.
Little smiling faces remind me
Of the joy that I lost
That was taken away
But I could not be
Forever young, forever free.
So I'll live my life
Longing.

Jennifer Fran Buhagiar
Gozo, Malta

Cast Shadow

Cold. So cold.
Got my mug between my hands
warming them.
I bend forward to feel
steam on nose.
I close my eyes and
you appear opposite me:

Your cigarette burning
in a cheap tin ashtray.
One hand gripping coffee
and the other thumbing through
Romeo and Juliet.
You smile while skimming lines of
loves' first meeting.

Me crying alone remembering
that night somewhere in my past
so vividly.
I smell damp pages.
I hear your voice breathe life
into words of an antiquated love story.
I see the corners of your lips
mandate the marionette sparkles of your eyes
to dance as you speak.

Me then in ecstasy.
My heart beating as that neon sign
flickers casting a pink shadow
through the window.

Me now in shock.
My eyes fixed on that empty chair.
Inside me love for you courses
through my body as
water through shattered flood gates.

You now my personal romantic hero.
Your last breath drawn and released
well before your time.
Me left with golden memories
and this cold, cold
emptiness I feel.

e. j. pauli
Ann Arbor, MI, , USA

Ask me

If you were to ask
    and if I had an answer

presupposing we had met
motive being dialogue
postulating your inclination to listen
and I not so reticent
    and apt to sarcasm

assuming complications had not distracted
hearing unobstructed by defenses
accepting you were interested
and I not so equivocal
    and prone to calenture

reckoning my voice rose above the din
not intentionally oblique
capturing dialogue uninterrupted
and you not so fragmented
    and loathe to details

I imagine you would find my explanation
slightly better than inadequate.

V. Holden
Houston, TX, USA

Friends--

Did you know I could hold a grudge
Without knowing you I can judge

I think I know it all
Standing puking in a stall
I'm the one about to fall

I'll take everything from you
and say things I know aren't true

I'm a bitch if you can't tell
My head's begun to swell
I'm not doing so well

I'll use up all of your stuff
And I'll never get enough

I love to go get high
I'll flirt with your favorite guy
And from all of this hate...

I'm about to die

"how I perceived my friend's point of view, after an argument"

Joelie Kuklis, age 17
Nebraska, USA

will you remember me?

will you remember me
when the cold winds blow
and wooden fingers tap
loudly against your window
waking you from
your peaceful slumber
will you remember me
when you dance in the rain
feeling the warm water
washing away
acidic memories
that burn with pain
will you remember me
when you see golden rays
falling from above
dancing on your face
caressing it softly
like a first lover
will you remember me
when the snow begins to fall
covering the earth
in a pure blanket
which you can happily
lose yourself in
will you remember me
when the cold winds blow
when the water falls
when the sun shines bright
when the snow falls
will you remember me?

Erin Love
Calgary, Alberta, Canada

I know of all the morphine, cocaine
and heroin that has ripped
through your veins

and when I dream
of seducing you
I pinch them and
kiss them
until they stand up
and tremble
at the notion of attention
after all these years
of being clean,
or so you say...

and when you finally fall asleep
I stay awake
running the tips of my fingers
over the rifts
that have become bigger
than the arms and legs
that they wind through

and an inkling of understanding
of the necessity
of your false charm
forces its way through me
from toe to head,
a syringe full of
methadone for a
virgin,
a synthetic lump of flesh
that listens,
for insomniac months and months
to the sound of your chest
rising and falling

Anik See
Stratford, Ontario, Canada

boundless

there is something
almost
beautiful
about it,

the
understanding acceptance
of the
load.

to embrace
it;
totally
and alone,
has a quality
rarely understood
by
any

excepting those,
who
have traveled
the
same
way.

Jason Smith
Church Crookham,
Fleet, England

Power

feeble hands hold strength like gold
and treasure what remains
grasping those fine fragments
of what was once their hope

they do not know the answer
and they do not care to hear
for what to them is of value which remains?
and what is left but fear?

i cannot be for them the strength they've banished
nor do they call my simple name
for it's not i they hate nor my life they cherish
not my useless words they long to know
i am but another, living there among
i do not know the question which first plagued them

and what is there to say of them without condemning?
what phrases or trite words have they not heard?
are they restless with excitement?
or simply broken souls chained like captives there?

i do not know
i cannot know
but wonder still
how a force which has no bounds, as power
could deceive even by its absence
and rule with but a whisper

Vanessa M. Brown
Lakeland, FL, USA

Little Charm School

(When the stress of Their regard
forced you to lock
your shivering little heart
within a box--
What did you learn?
Exactly what
was the cost?)

I Learned to
Distrust the motive
and
Suspect the vow.
(You never could
count on them, anyhow!)

I Questioned the
Necessity to feel

and the
Drive to need.
(Oh, we all know what complications
those two can breed!)

I Believed that
Even in a
loving heart
Mediocrity could
breed contempt.
(They are far and few
for whom that fact is exempt!)

I Know it cost me
my Heart,
my Comfort,
my Deep sense of Right.
(Well, what can One say, My Dear?
It's left you with one Hell of a life.)

Amanda Estes "Valkyroi"
Vallejo, CA, USA

Personal String Theory

Across a moonlit parking-lot
The sparse winds of mid-winter blow pieces
Of crumpled paper and ruined leaves to eternity
While in the distance an engine starts.

A cloud of frozen exhaust gives away the
Starting point of one lone night traveler
And I see the red and white of her tail-lights
As she backs away, leaving a blank space

Between the rows of cars. There is a place
Now, a connection, where she is forever
Just going and I am forever watching, forever
About to look up into the expanse of stars and

Think how very like a star she is to me; remote
And unknowable. Like the static light images
That flow from stars, she and I forever expanding
Into greater and greater circles, together, alone,

Outward and away from one another.
Or do we here now shrink into the future?
That's just relative, I suppose. Either way I end
Up here in the frozen parking lot, wind battered.

*"…in physics, string theory is the attempt to `unite' all forces of nature…
perhaps we also attempt `unification'…
even if it turns out cold and static"*

David B. Donlon
Alexandria, VA, USA

SURRENDER !

Where the sea whispers
Hear my Voice,
Where the rains fall
Taste my tears
Where the thunder storms
Bear my Fears.

Wherever you look,
Whatever you see,
Whenever you feel
the Joy,
the Pain,
the Sorrow,
Beware !
They carry my name.
I gave them birth
and was born by them.
I am the parent
and the child
I am the queen
and the maid

I am the change
and the same
I am
and
I am not.
I live in your dreams,
In your silence,
In your screams.
I am filled by you
And I fill your senses
With the whispering seas,
The Destroyer of Fences !

Surrender !

*"we pretend the world consists of
isolated entities, but the fences exist
only in our minds"*

Nena Sudar
Zagreb, Croatia

Distorted

Why does everything
Have to be
Distorted,

Slammed through an overdrive pedal
By an insane guitarist
Screwing with the chords

And a nutball Bass player
playing it all flat?

Visions of sunny days
Ripped apart by black paint
Thrown on by a blind artist
Who can't feel the colours,

Perspectives changed
By myopic glasses
On a girl
Who can't see what's in front of her.

I've been wasting my time for so long
Trying to figure out the chords
But always getting E#
As the answer,

But it only takes a second of silence
A wrong pedal push
To move to a clear tone
With a bit of chorus,

Just enough time
For the sound to clear the speakers
And the flashing lights to stop
In the corner of the haze-filled room.

"life can be deceptive, but also frighteningly clear"

Hayden Griffiths-Johnson, age 17
Christchurch, New Zealand

For Violeta   *(transl. Vyt Bakaitis)*

There's nothing more, only a nightingale in frost
sobbing for resurrection, only the wild
pansy waiting around for dawn. Nothing
other than the light studying a face
through dawn-struck drawn curtains.

There's nothing, other than footprints in a map
of dunes, a railway network to the east.
Nothing more. And it's not worth seeing past
the limits of poverty: a faded summer survives
to endure winter in highway billboard shields.

Nothing else. But is it worth hoping?
Processions of despair climb the stairs
of early dawn, coming closer. There's nothing else.
For sure? A sand-castle on the beach
quivers with the newborn, as yet unwashed morning.

Nothing more. Rowboats with lowered hands
and bees in frost-embedded hives breaking
into tears. Nothing but this. Just a subdued
Miles Davis allowing a slight breather
to turn the freezing page over.

*"for this generation, so split up, vulgarized, clipped, made dizzy with all the grime
clouding body and soul, the task of poetry is to revive and raise the individual and
draw him or her, as far as possible, into the amazing, many-faceted and all-but-
incredible world of language"*

Julius Keleras
New York, NY, USA / Vilnius, Lithuania

REGARDING YOUR SON

Who is now seventeen
Who is now a rebel
Who is now just
out of reach
of you.

Regarding your son
who is now growing scar tissue
who is now learning the world
you taught him
doesn't necessarily work.

Regarding your son,
there is nothing I can tell you
now
that he hasn't already.

C. C. Russell
Wheatland, WY, USA

Joan of Arc

I'm not comforted by the concept of your faithfulness
I'm not settled by the thought of your reward.
I'm not better with the promise of a paradise
And I don't believe it's gonna be alright.

We're all running from our champions to escape our satisfaction
We don't want to understand the universe and what it holds
Sometimes we need a role to play, sometimes we want to fade away

So I raise my fists to the demon beast of my identity
And beg for a reality that doesn't end this way.
Sweet Joan of Arc, if I pretend to understand
Will you flatter me with dignity and lead me on to grace?

I'm not afraid to accept that I'm a villain
I'm just afraid that I'll have nothing to accept.
If I spend eternity as someone's cruel antagonist
Will I still have you to reach for when eternity ends?

None of us are eclectic, none of us are apolitical
None of us fight for justice quite as hard as for our greed
Or perhaps you are all good, perhaps I have misunderstood,
        perhaps I am the only bad guy here

I say my prayers to the patron saint of selfishness
And ask God for forgiveness for all the things I want
Sweet Joan of Arc, if I tithe and read your tale tonight
Will you stand there with your sword when I'm alone and in the dark?

I'm far away now from the things that I hold sacred
From my ties and my obsessions, from the fetishes I don't appreciate
Don't lie to me, I know that I'm not wanted
Let's not pretend I'm here for my benefit

I dry my tears and curse God for all my faithlessness
While trying to convince myself that I have yet to sin
Sweet Joan of Arc, if I stab my demons in the back
Will I have your understanding when my virtues grow thin?

Jonathan Penton
Marietta, GA, USA

Someone Does It Better

And, though tough, we just have to accept
that our dear labor, our cherished
soufflés, hand-carved banisters,
or well turned-jokes
are lofted, notched and spun by those,
to whom, they mean nothing.
There should be a sympathy between longing
and skill, so true plumbers
would love nothing like the smell
of flux and those with song
would have pipes of sliver.
But no, someone now, as we read,
lovelessly makes what we hold most dear,
and we, us, you and I
are left to watch them make it well.

R. J. McCaffery
Providence, RI, USA

RUNNING DOWN
FROM THE DAYS
ON SUBURBAN ASPHALT
WAS A CHILDHOOD
CERTAINTY
WHEN TIME WAS
DEFINED BY ACTIVITY
ALONE
WITH NO NOD
TO ANY PROGRESSION
BEYOND BREAKFAST,
LUNCH AND DINNER
AND THE PRIMETIME TV LINEUP.
EACH DAY A COMPLETE EPISODE
THROUGH THESE MARKERS
SET IN PLACE
BY HOUSEWIVES AROUND
OUR COMINGS AND GOINGS
WELL-DRESSED CLOCKHANDS
FUELED BY SUGAR AND
EARLY BEDTIMES
DESTINED TO GROW
INTO PEOPLE
WHO EAT AT
ODD HOURS

Jennifer M. Boudreaux
Portland, ME, USA

nothing's changed

we're supposed to care
about certain things
-now it's okay to
vote and
work and
fight
it's okay to never shave
but its not okay
to not care-
nothing's really changed

they know what we are
but lets not let on
that we know
that they know
what we're glad they know
but aren't supposed to notice.
they might rape us
they might scar us
or they might just like the forbidden fruit

so take it all into careful consideration
before you dress each day
my mother says
well I've considered
and they've never noticed me before
and if they do now, then I'll know why
but I like the seldom freedom
of a sleeveless shirt
and I don't care anymore

so they may rape us and scar us
or just enjoy the sight of the forbidden fruit
-we all do

and I've scarred myself
deeply enough
trying to do it all just right

and they'll rape us anyway
they'll always rape us

so nothing's changed mom
nothing changed,
so why should I?

S. N., age 16
Saline, MI, USA

Messenger

"Who are you?" asked a stranger of me
I am death and dreams abandoned
I am the darkest night in the lightest soul
I am despair and rage unchecked
I've come to burn the truth into all who would hear
Change your ways oh son of Sodom
God has eyes and ears to hear
The pain and suffering he sees
Is given to me to bare
And to you...to witness
Seek a new path
Salvation is not what you should fear
But the unattended tear

Paul S. Williams
Rohnert Park, CA, USA

CHAINS

Outside time in a private hell
No reality in present
Past and future alive
Put this pain to rest
I am now deep inside

Clock stopped
For a tremor of the heart
Stillness, peace
Reclamation of the beast
Give me back my instincts
This is sensation
Heart bursting, blood quickening
I am alive
Creator and destroyer
Eat of meat and taste its soul
Like the grass I grow
A prayer for the dying
Blood lust, hunger, passion sated
I crave and seek salvation
Let me smell the land
Lead me through the garden
By my hedonism
Whilst my hands are bound
I cannot touch
Eternally damned
In my dark room, the light within
Mind's eye against the blindness
This is only half of living
Drowned in a river of time

"about depression...how the mind is everywhere but the here-and-now,
leading to lost emotions and a sense of being two-dimensional"

Clare Avory
Bradford, West Yorkshire, England

You Must Love Me

You have to do more
than just open your eyes,
if you want to see me.
You have to do more
than just understand,
if you want to know me.

It is not enough to
just be silent and listen,
if you want to hear me.
You must love me,
if you want me to be
heard, known and seen.

You have to do more
to be there for me,
than just hold my hand.
It is not enough
to know where I am,
to just look at the ground I stand on
For I am not always where I seem,
and you must love me,
to know of the things I dream.
And you must love me,
to see me inside,
for that's where I am,
and that's what I hide.

And you must love me,
to know why
I'm childish and wise.
And you must love me,
to hear
the things I speak through my eyes.
And you must love me,
to understand
how I feel.
Then you will know how
to help me heal,
- you must love me.

*"wanting to be understood...love is an essential to reach deep into
a person's real being"*

Deborah C. B. Greco
Terrigal, NSW, Australia

Darkness

I find myself alone again,
the darkness is my only friend.
She envelopes me in her arms
and never lets me come to harm.
She holds me close and blinds my eyes
and now she is my best disguise,
from dealing with my pain inside
when really I just want to hide,
and never feel the burning pain
that's almost driving me insane.
So hold me close, my dearest friend
and never make me feel again.

*"in the dark, staring at my computer screen, I just started writing,
my wish never to feel loneliness again"*

Jada Marie Andrews , *age 17*
Mt. Pleasant, MI, USA

A Flame Rises Darkly

Winter thaws
it's illusions melting to reveal
not men but statues beneath the snow.
A flame rises darkly
out from years of time cracked stone.
An alien in this nocturne.
The crowd is rusty and unfed
but you move between their clasping hands
with swift and confident movements.
Life incarnate.
They fear your refining fire
as it crackles in searing bursts around you.

*"the decline of the old system,
the emergence of a New Age"*

Alexander Wallis
Southbourne, Emsworth, England

("thinking our way out of Here")

pensivity is so DULL
    the barely-flicker of a muted television.
    peripheral hallucinations, tiptoeing shadows
    who have names if we think to give them.
        DON'T BLINK he says &
        i analyze for what he meant;
    stare ahead to see the Truth of a future
    the washy colours of inadequacy & uncertainty
    are the blindingest ones. i want to EAT THEM UP!
        full of idea
        what else makes the humans live so long?
    America the Bored:

    we are the least of it,
        EX-PATRIOTS
        SHIT-TALKERS
        TV-BABY,
    oh child   i cry out the window
    to myself, THINK & be free
    but don't think too hard,
America the Pensive

we are high & stuck.

Christina Gay
Baltimore, MD, USA

intermezzo

Plum is the voice of evensong
intermezzo over unsung phrases of day;
when septet tunes and turns a page

then stage belongs to a lone nocturne
intermezzo over unsung phrases of day.
Silence is briefly an inwrought song;

then stage belongs to a lone nocturne
sung by birds who have nested and gone.
Silence is briefly an inwrought song

as played by oboes that have no reed,
sung by birds who have nested and gone
on declining stars in rising dawn;

as played by oboes that have no reed.
When septet tunes and turns a page
on declining stars in rising dawn
plum is the voice of evensong.

"moments passed at the cusp of transitional measures of time"

Marc Awodey
Burlington, VT, USA

ONCE UPON A TIME
THEY UNDERSTOOD EACH OTHER'S WORDS
WITHOUT SAYING.

ONCE UPON A TIME
THEY TOUCHED EACH OTHER'S HEARTS
WITHOUT BEING CLOSE.

ONCE UPON A TIME
THEY SAW EACH OTHER'S THOUGHTS
WITHOUT LOOKING

TODAY
THEY DESPERATELY TRY
TO UNDERSTAND,
REACH OUT,
AND SEE
THINGS THAT, ONCE UPON
WERE THE AIR THEY BREATHED
AS ONE!

"love was once an emotion so strong that words were needless...but has now become an emotion where words are useless"

Nena Sudar
Zagreb, Croatia

SUICIDE INSIDE:

feel me sink into your flesh
I'm the dagger drawn by death
feel me grow within your womb
I'm the soldier wielding doom
feel me sufficing carnal needs
I'm the self implanted seed
        the dread who's never freed
        the path which nowhere leads

feel me spit on all thou hast
I'm the broken childhood past
feel me keep love out of range
I'm the path of all estranged
feel me crush your hopes and dreams
I'm the sun which never gleams
        the night of endless screams
        the sorrow's reign supreme

I, within your mind,
am love and loss entwined.
The absence one shall find,
in barren hopes denied,
which shall not subside...
until your suicide.

Richard Scott Carter
Marquette, MI, USA

Flipside

I. Poet

The drunk at the end of the war
says words are built to pimp–
poetry is a sucker punch line
that sets you up with a caress
and knocks you down a flight
of stares from swing-shift
waitresses who have better
things to lose than dignity.

This one's fed up.
She squints at the neon
curve in a barstool and wipes
the table down with a comic strip,
its inky narrative following her
home in a folded apron
to little hands and silly putty imprints.

Soon the kid loses interest
or imagination and he buries
the strip aside, its putty ghost
stretched and distorted
on the refrigerator until it dries.

In ten years, everything dries.
                Kid takes off.
Says mothers bent to tend bar
before scraped knees deserve
an empty nest.

II. Word

The shifts swing slower
now that the streets gleam
more inviting. And she's out there
like a melodrama, taking curb
strides with her head so high
it's detached. Not quite angels,
the lamp posts bow down
to her glide, and when she kisses
her crucifix it tastes more like copper
than any ash-lined tip jar.

The drunk, she thinks; He's doing this.
From that cracked vinyl
and squeaky pivot, he's out
of body and into her stocking,
pulling on a loose thread
until it's long enough for a leash–
or a noose, when it's convenient.

III. Poem

He's probably got the kid
in some boxcar or sympathetic breadline,
telling priests his mom's a whore
and he can't help it.

Or maybe he's slouching
in a Boston bus station
at three a.m., watching a monitor
rerun with a sitcom star who talks
to the camera like we're in on the joke.

For the pulse of a stoplight
she senses this, then peels
off a shard of paper blown
against her thigh–the flipside
of the funny pages laments
her beery prophet's obituary:

He choked to death on a corndog
while heckling the circus,
but not before He broke
into the big top and proved absurdity,
when placed between two funhouse
mirrors, casts an echo that never fades away.

Jeremy Hoffart
Spokane, WA, USA

diluted

the sounds are stained,
diluted, but resonating
from within, like the
sound after really loud

music, and i'm trying
to sleep, but it's constant
and my heart beats
faster, liquefying my

thoughts, which are
somehow diluted and
transparent, i think
the sky swallowed my

ambition and left me
to wallow, mesmerized
by the onlookers, who
can see straight through

me, for i am transparent
now, and they can hear
my diluted noise, see my
diluted thoughts, so why

aren't they laughing,
their indifference
is frightening, and
for some reason my

tear goes unnoticed,
as does my silence,
and my emotion used
to be who i was, but now

i can't find the strength,
which is detrimental
to everything, because hell
is not hot, it's become diluted like me.

Erik Yannuzzi
Harlem, GA, USA

even now as I wait

streetlights change.
The coffee is slow in coming
from an owner wanting tips.
A short hair blonde flashes
her pretty small pink breasts
for the hell of it.
These are the moments
the ones worth waiting for
…they just happen.
I sip the java
she smiles
knowing what I am thinking
as you
probably know.
Doctor say
I should quit smoking
quit drinking coffee and tea
one asked about
drugs and drinking
they want me to quit
who i am
who am I
to quit living…
one day
it'll just
happen
like
tears
on a lonely face.

L. S. Shevshenko
Macon, GA, USA

familyplanning

they've sunk you in that dunk tank
of religion again, hoping hoping it's
just a so-called phase, that you'll
soon hop that woman-chasin' train
to wedville and pop out some blue-
eyed intelligentsia. and your brother
aims and whoosh, you're down again.

they want Sears portraits for mantel
jewelry. they want copies and copies
of their gene pool, the comeuppance of
middle american success. they'll sink you like
a witch though. and if you'll capitulate
they'll relent and find you ms. perfectblonde
with a degree in doting. yes dear no
dear sure dear. sex? dinner? this
dress? i'll fetch...that's SO cute.

they want you to "keep your options
open." perhaps inhibit yourself
to one night a week — it's GAY DAY at
Wrigley field, and if you're good
you can keep the mementos tucked
in that locked familiar closet.

come on son. take it. it's that
good ole boy drug. not too much now
or you'll kill yourself. we'll
help you become...and you'll like it.
step on up.

with those tincan hands they cut you
so deep boy. and when you bled
it was all simple, more than pure —
a bump on old mama fascist pride —
a comma to remember who you are
when the water's shrunk and their
trump's worn thin.

Heather L. Igert
St. Louis, MO, USA

STRANGE LOVE

It's not fair for me to
expect you to make
me real,
to create a place
for you and I ... untouched and pure.
I wanted to find a warm spot,
to curl up in it and hide.
Disappear from you and your world
which you shut me out of
but flaunted in my face.
A world I desperately wanted to belong to
but only slipped along the edges.
Now I look at you
and see a faint glimmer in your eyes,
sending shivers down my spine,
because for a brief moment
I have a memory of our world
but it fades a quickly as your eyes
drift away from mine.

Stacey MacWilliam
Hamiton, Ontario, Canada

Counting the cost in advance
I won't take you up
Won't dance all night
Not again.
I can almost taste
What it felt like to run
So fast
To see the sun rise
Reflecting its rays in your eyes
What a waste of sublime
Gestures of love
You don't mean for me -
Either you
Or I
Must go out of my mind.

Dena Bugel-Shunra
Tel-Aviv, Israel

Here lies tomorrow

Tonight
the rain falls
the angels sing
how beautiful fate is,
fate, and living,
wanting to kiss the clouds
that saved me from myself
and from your nature
in the cold night.
Nothing else
matters but tomorrow's sorrow
and i fear that without you...it follows me
with my rain and tears
and i ache inside
to think i cannot accept or understand
all the love you offer and
bring to my heart
and i wonder
while the day passes
and moon comes to listen to my
cries
the mountain air whispers of change coming
while looking with weary eyes
i turn
to where my heart first left to be with yours
and i follow
Goodnight child,
here leaves
tomorrow's sorrow.

"in the midst of loss and grief, experiencing love for the first time...
change softening the sorrow"

Shanterrian Green
Columbia, SC, USA

He

fucks me in the morning, before
the sun has risen and then leaves
without saying a word   he is
distant all day and stumbles
in for dinner four hours late
so drunk he can barely speak
or keep his eyes open, skirting
around me   he opens another beer
the one that will make him
resentful and angry, i know,
has a sip and starts in on the
same speech i've heard a million
times in the two months i've known
him   he's happy, he says, but i don't
know jackshit about his problems so
why don't i just stick to my own
little pathetic uppity life and go fuck
myself because he's getting off this bus
god has special plans for him where he's going
holding his finger like a gun to his head   POW
he goes outside to smoke his last cigarette and
leaves,
as usual.

Anik See
Stratford, Ontario, Canada

TITLED

O'Neill, in joy, got good and lit
The day they changed his title to
"Executive Associate
Consultant, Revenue."

Now he gets jacked each night and day
Since Rawlinson received the name
"The Special Lead Advisor to the Pay-
Roll System Analyst of Burlingame."

With syllabic validation
Six empty beats will outrank five.
In the quibble for verbal inflation
Only the long survive.

Joseph Kenny
San Francisco, CA, USA

Mirrored Soul

Please. Close the door.
Welcome to your own darkness
Not afraid are you ?
Surely, it's just your true self
Look here at your black soul
Stinking and desecrated
And here, a cold heart
Always the bastard.
Like you say
They like it that way
Now what ?
I hear you ask
Through your fetid lips
Shit is all you speak
Your mouth is an anus
In this glorious world
A world not of your putrescence
But of hope and love.
You've taken what your balls wanted
Now leave us in peace.
Time to die.

Phil Steadman
Stafford, England

Insanity

I nearly lost it
took a step too far
took a leap too short
and was pushed
all in one
for life
into insanity
pulling
and
scratching
my
way
back
has not
left me sane

Cathrine Lødøen
Oslo, Norway

Mind and Soul

A balance
That's what I seek
But often the mind is too strong
And the soul too weak

What I wouldn't give
For my soul to run the show
Telling my mind
The places to go

Sometimes I get there
To that blissful plain
Often it's the only time
I truly feel sane

Maybe I push too hard
To achieve this lofty goal
Pushing aside my mind
And just listening to my soul

I do believe
That someday very soon
My mind will forever step aside
And my soul will swoon

Soaring ever higher
All the way to the stars
Joyfully crying out
Finally, freed from my bars

"one cannot find `self' when worrying
how we're perceived by others"

Brian Ehrhardt
Spokane, WA, USA

Send in the Clowns

i wanna quit school i wanna drop out
i wanna lock myself in the
basement with a mag lite and a
black roller ball pen so i can
write poetry in the semi-dark
all over the god-damn walls. i wanna
write all day or is it night it's all the
same down here. doen't matter never come out
live on processed cheese and giggle all the time
because surprise! i finally lost my fucking mind.
jump around like a monkey snort the fumes from
the ez-cheez can gotta get that buzz somehow.
need someone to fuck so i'll have something
to write about.
send down a man i'll send him back when i'm done
fucking and writing 'til someone dies
probably not me i should be so lucky.
need some inspiration send in the clowns i'll
fuck them too and the best part,
the best part is that it will be okay. no one will mind.
people will say "she's eccentric" can you believe that,
eccentric. and we all know eccentricity
breeds genius right? fucking genius.

isn't that shit crazy? i know what i'm gonna do
i'm gonna start a cult. that'll piss 'em off.
a pagan cult with me as an absentee god
because i'm still in the basement and
once a year when there's a quarter moon i'm gonna
gather all my followers together on the lawn
and i'm gonna leave my shit-hole basement
and come outside where all my followers await
the blessing of my presence.
and you know what i'm gonna do? i'm gonna
scratch my crotch and spit on the lawn and
then go back to my basement.
and my followers, they'll eat that shit up.
because that's what they do, they follow.
maybe i'll sell tickets. you wanna be my follower
you gotta buy a ticket. buy a ticket so you
can stand on my lawn and maybe catch a
glimpse of me scratching. maybe you'll be lucky
maybe i'll spit on you. but you better believe
you're gonna pay more for a ticket
within spitting range 'cuz hey, I am your
God, after all. And damn, is that ever gonna piss
off the right wing christian coalition Motherfuckers
because only their God can charge people a fee
to be spit on.

Audrey Rae Shangle
Ann Arbor, MI, USA

you and i

you and i
could be like
thelma and louise
we could really
escape these walls
they don't have to
close in on us

and you could write
christmas cards for a living
employed by hallmark
you know, the money ain't
so bad

and we could be happy
just to sit close together
in a mansion in beverly hills

and i could go to work
for the Galleria
some top exec
come home w/ a check of
several hundred
a week
and we could be the picture perfect
imitation
of heterosexuality

somehow i think
i don't want that
i'm ready for vengeance
i'm ready to shoot
i think i'd rather tear down
these walls
than decorate them with macromet
or whatever the latest fad is

you and i
we could try
to be lavern and shirley
living the american women's dream
or we could be outlaws
and die a tragic death

you and i
prisoners of the weaker sex
we'll never escape
no matter which way we run
it'll be the same
as pretending
because i remember
i forgot the ending
they die
either we're miserable and we live
or we run
then we finally give up
and we kill ourselves
to save us from surrender
well i got news—we surrendered
the days we were born.

"I am NOT `a normal girl who just
happens to be gay'...I'd rather suffer
hardships to be who I am than pretend
to be something I'm not"

M. Anna
Phoenix, AZ, USA

Family

The father made himself
another cocktail
of tranquilizers and rye,
trying to reach
some tiny spot

of excruciating pain,

pin it down
like an elusive bulls-eye.

He missed yet again
and called up his daughter
letting his grief
run wild,

letting it flatten
even the smallest flower
of her day

letting it pile up high
on her back

and form

a pleasure dome.

"a father's relief, his raging
confessions of misery, his
daughter's burden"

Andrea Nicki
Montreal, Quebec, Canada

Maybe tomorrow

I've had more than my share of ill luck.
My days are all cloudy and
The sun doesn't care to shine through
To set free my sorrow.
Maybe tomorrow.

I can't walk straight on the roads of time.
I move forward, but keep slipping back,
Skidding on sands left behind by others.
Is there any happiness I can borrow?
Maybe tomorrow.

My boat is lost in stormy seas
And the sky & stars my only friends.
I'm thirsty even as the rain falls around me.
If only someone could help me row.
Maybe tomorrow.

On my track the sun's never shone.
I'm hungry for love, that I've never known.
I wait for a harvest that's never been sown.
Tell me when and tell me how,
Maybe tomorrow, Lord, but why not now?

Anand Subramanian
Patna, Bihar, India

I've gotten used to the madness
now I get lonely when it is sane.
There ain't no difference between the silence of nothing
and the silence of noise,
they make me lonely just the same.

Emma Anderson, age 18
Figtree, NSW, Australia

You Drive Joy into my Heart

I used to die,
depressingly slowly, in a dismal
domain, submerged
in a vale of black.
My pain was eternal,
like the life of a vampire,
though it was not confined to night.
It made day night for me.
How I wished I could live,
then I met you,
You drove joy into my heart.

You slew
my dejection, brought light
to my world, through
your incandescent eyes. Resurrected,
I now live in your world,
it passes too quickly,
an eternity
seems like a second
in your company
yet every one is a precious
capsule of sensation to be stored
forever.

You;
you are the epitome of beauty,
perfection incarnate.
An aura of ecstasy
emanates from your presence
your voice is melodic
Every time I see you,
You drive joy into my heart.

You;
you do not know the feelings you evoke
and you may never for I,
I am terrified of rejection.

Rejection
would harden my heart, turn day
back to night.
I would die slowly again.
My harder heart would protect
my depression from slaying
by you, or another.
I would be dead forever.

So I glow
silently in your presence,
hoping that the feelings you evoke,
however unlikely, are mutually provoked
by us both, and that you would comprehend
and act, then truly you,
You would drive joy into my heart.

Russell Ainslie
Westhill, Scotland

The shooting star I hopped,
cruised on back to club eternity
(from The Inconvenience of Beauty)

Flinging the doors wide I moved
like a black cat to the counter, eyed
the jester playing his pipes and said,
"make mine a double!"

He lifted the glass remarked "your Desire?"
"To inspire" I replied,
"To reveal the hidden sparkle in all things!"

The inconvenient con; he laughed filling
the glass to pass across the counter, beside
his own. Two objects orbiting, suddenly meet
with gentle chiming mockery to the sweet ironic universe ways,
"two for the road" he said,
as the clock struck none...

"dedicated to anyone who does not fit the mold of the merely practical, or useful"

Anni Paisley
Burlington, VT, USA

IF YOU ASK ME

Hey soul sista, keep your head up high;
Don't let anyone tell you, you can't claim the prize;

I've seen your struggle, I've tasted your tears;
I've watched you lay down and pretend you weren't there;

I've seen you beat down and battered, weary and weak;
Cracked out and coked up by some trick you meet;

All alone in the alley freezing from the rain;
Because the money's out, it's moving time again;

Through all this one might speculate;
Label you "hype" past redemption state;

But little do they know,

One night quarter past 10;
You asked God for forgiveness
And started life again;

"society has given up on its most precious tool -
the power to call on the will of God"

Kareemah El-Amin
South Bend, IN, USA

Religion

A broken sail is a pole in the sand
That once was the bottom – now is the top,
Blue depths of dead seas that no one sees,
The wind with no smell of sparkling waves.

It is the religion of the following days –
The wind with no smell of sparkling waves.

The smoke disappears, revealing a trench;
I hoped it was mist over a field,
Lost in limitless wasteland drained of life
A farm by the field with a mountain of hay.

It is the religion of the following days –
A farm by the field with a mountain of hay.

Disputes over who should carry the blame
For dead yellow seas, for blood soaked fields
Don't matter to Earth drying its tears
With a burning sunset after rain in May.

It is the religion of the following days.
A burning sunset after rain in May.

"inspired by environmental disasters such as the drying Aral Sea,
and wars such as the conflict in Chechnya"

Andrey Y. Morozov, age 20
Moscow, ID, USA/St. Petersburg, Russia

Fast Talker

You were always
such
Pomp and Circumstance--
A well matched graffiti
Of self -knowledge
           -love
-loathing
that still owes nothing,
knows nothing
of any process but it's own.

Always Oh soooo
charming, disarming.
Perfectly timing that terrible wit
--remembering Just when to grin a bit—
Starting…
           Stopping///
Drawing them in--
twisting facts into fictions
with wild predictions
and
twinkle-eyed comebacks
that are
leading, speeding
toward an auto-wrecked truth.

Glib! Fib! The Bloody cut of your Jib!

Give us all
        An eyeful.
                An earful.

They do so dearly

Love-love-love you!

Rubbernecking for their glimpse
of the artful pileup
that is
your shifty imagination.

Amanda Estes "Valkyroi"
Vallejo, CA, USA

The First to Fall into Sleep

A freight train bellowed from faraway
over tatters of freezing sunset.
Home and cars in this perplexing valley
have become grounded reminders of stars.

Let me be the first to fall into sleep
under linen November bedclothes,
for I have seen too much today
to hope to gaze into livid evening.

Each century is oppressively chimerical;
and gaudiness is mistaken for radiance.
I am a son among a million bewildered sons
who haunt quiet, productive wastelands.

Let me be the first to fall into sleep
for I have seen too much today.

"from a nihilistic view of epochal change…a search for context"

Marc Awodey
Burlington, VT, USA

Wet and Dying Under a Singular Sun

she's wet and dying under a singular sun
　　with her hair strewn about her
　　　　with tangle-like impressions and folk music,
like being here before the tide of the moment
　　　　in plural monstrosity chambered and sick
　　　　and fierce all at once with mesmerizing
　　　　silkiness.
the way in which motion is E-motion
　　　　a singular notion discounting dysfunction
　　　　and walled in and closed boxes
　　　　like cardboard arteries only made in the U.S.A.
forgive and forget, she told me alive in the sand
　　　　with tweaking purity unscarred honesty
　　　　and a tequila in the other hand offering
　　　　silence.
for now alive seems best with ice and shot glasses
　　　　somehow never seems far away and waving
　　　　expecting with boredom a silkiness undiscovered
　　　　untouched and ferocious in white black and grey
　　　　with color strewn about that singular sun,
　　　　wet and dying.

"the extremes and unextremes of patience and waiting"

Travis Talley, age 20
Mulberry, FL, USA

The Rope that Hangs

The love in my heart
has become my blanket
my wall, my rope
bearing upon my soul

The war on drugs is on
The television blares this lie
like a bugle on a Sunday morning wake up call
My country has evaporated from sweet water ocean
to maggot infested sand
Where the American Dollar can purchase
a new born baby fresh with umbilical cord
and uncut cocaine
straight from the colon
of our newest courier

We're winning the war on drugs
Write that on Miguel's headstone
who just couldn't say no
to the four "G's" a week
he was clocking
for dropping caps up the corner
and down the street
where he was met with a nine
and ripped open
so his intestines could do the sidewalk dance
and his backup could take his cut

Winning the war on drugs
It seems easier to block the passage
of Immigrants willing to work in sweatshops
Than to block the passage
of drug dealing diplomats
whose staff is always in the toilet

The country of my Father's birth grows it
The country of my birth buys it
So to escape this nightmare
I hold onto the love in my heart
It has become my wall, my blanket, my rope

It gives me strength
to help people awaken
from the sleep of the pipe
At the same
Turn from cold turkey reality
to the reality of minimum wage

This is the rope that hangs me
I can only offer the love in my heart
as a blanket
my garden of growth for nourishment
and the knowledge of hope, strength, and self-love
as a rope to hold onto

E. G. Cortés
Newburgh, NY, USA

"You there"

Do you feel it?-   that time to be?
-as if it were noon and dying?
~ to be that girl on the street six days a week
selling powdered cakes for a place to be at home
where there are no pastries
to be smelled
~ to be that symphonic Arabian horse beating pounding
in A minor pondering to the horizon
on ivory and onyx keys
that sparkle and jump
~ to be that howdy junky smoking Buddha in the cemetery
dreaming on God -   fogged over memories
of the red head from Baltimore
whose eyes burned deeper than he could see
~ to be that fag and to know your brother like a sister
-finding a dream behind a pants zipper
that points its way to truth
and infinity in eight inches
~ to be that guy in the camel pack
standing tall and proud, elbows and shoulders back
-erect as the leg, the crutch
that carries him
~ to be so present that you are counted...

and not forgotten in the smoke
while the flame spits and burns
~ to be the first soul to appear in a Polaroid
of the banal- a crow standing
on a tombstone
~ to feel and know the figures in your head
-counted and stockpiled
but never spoken to in public
~ to know love in the early morning-   naked and
binding our hands, speaking in tongues
from ancient depth, as we are married
under the moon
~ to feel the distance between two places
like it were the edges of a mole,
chronicled and measured for an increase in size
-the tell tale signs of cancer
~ to know love as a poet and hate it
-for it stultifies your only power,
the words which are useless in defining
its presence and strength

~ to see life- not drunk, not sober and more
than the cyclical existences...

Oh, what treasures in heaven and hell may equal
age's youth and to know the being of life, of love?
I question you, kind sir, as you
pause to straighten the penny in your shoe
and lick your hand to flatten your hair.

Sean Casey
Hudson, NY, USA

Sweet euphoric peace of mind
Control my life and my time
Always leave me feeling fine
Until the ride is over
Visions floating graceful by
Winged serpents cross the sky
Cannot see them though I try
I am herded by the drover
All my will is lost to sin
My lusts and desires always win
As sweet temptation drags me in
The passion's growing stronger
My strongest thoughts can't rescue me
They're locked within my fantasy
And sensation numbed by ecstasy
I own myself no longer
And when my skin begins to crawl
And cravings wrap me in a ball
For sweet temptation do I call
To take away my pain
And take me to a better land
Were I can make another stand
And live delusions oh so grand
Until the feeling starts to wane.

"some become lost within their `escape' to such depth that the escape becomes
more powerful than reality...I have lost friends consumed in such escapes"

Raymond D. Lamb
Elizabeth Grove, South Australia

My Best Friend

Best friends we were
Lifelong companions we are
Always in my heart
And from my mind not far

I remember the times we had
The lasting memories and a dream
I loved her like a sister
Together forever or so it would seem

The days of hanging out
The phone calls that lasted forever
The Thursday night keyboard lessons
The things we had to discover

Her last birthday
Spent at the beach
Writing names in the sand
The sunset crimson and peach

Endless days I hold so dear
That nothing can replace
And the thought of her death
Still makes my heart race

I lost something I never knew I had
A best friend, a sister, a Guardian Angel
And with a tear in my heart
I look at the situation from every angle

She was a part of me
With her brown hair and shiny eyes
But now she's a part of the night breeze
And with her the twinkling stars hold the same ties

I'll always remember my Missy
And all those carefree days
In my heart she will live forever
"Stand by Me" was our phrase

"my best friend died when we were only 14, and her death affected me greatly"

April Stuck, age 18
Rixford, PA, USA

Consciences, going cheap!!!

Hello consumers
customers, shoppers
As, Bs, maybe Cs
(forget the Ds and Es)
what can we sell you today?

How about this back?
One owner only,
but many masters
No longer needed
as the owner is unemployed

The first twenty callers
will get a set of
Twisted, scarred fingers
FOR FREE! CALL NOW!

Or maybe you'd like
a guaranteed job for life
these are handy little numbers
very hard to find
available to valued clients
good luck required
satisfaction not included

not interested?
(a quizzical look)

how about this item?
we don't sell many
can't figure why they're here
terribly old-fashioned
very clumsy and heavy
can cause pain and discomfort
they require humility and respect
however there are some good features
it comes with a built in crap-detector
and provides years of good feeling

I'll take it,
it's just what I've been looking for!

So, would you like a bag
for your social conscience?

*"listen to any broadcast and count how many times
our multi-faceted lives are reduced to mere consumption"*

Darren Jones
Clarence Park, South Australia

The Forest of Shadows

Like fools in the dark you make your way through
The forest of shadows.
Ghastly-deformed trees and vines grab at you
From above and behind.
Mother Nature showed you the way home but you
In your blindness took the path your ignorant ancestors
Claimed as the way to Shangri-La...
The way to total bliss and perfect happiness
Where there is no sickness or hunger, no hatred!
Everyone is equal and there is no such thing as different.
You thought everything there would be brilliant!
A halo on every child's head and on every cloud
A silver lining.
But, you were wrong everything is gray,
And the rain falls day and night.
You didn't realize what makes you special is your differences.
Your sickness and hunger make you strong not weak,
Because you overcame the sickness and feed the hunger.
There is no harmony in total equality; just a simple melody
That repeats its boring phrase over and over.
Without the hatred there is no love.
Shangri-La is nature's hell, and so I will not take the beaten path.
I seek earth, not a mythical heaven with its twisted nirvana.
I will live in reality with human thoughts and human feelings.
I am not infallible, but I am one of God's perfect beings.
My diverse heritage is my gift,
And being different does not make me a freak!
I will follow Mother Nature home, and there I will find peace.
I will right the wrongs you started.
I will lead my descendents away from the forest,
And the slow death it creates as it spreads to engulf us all.
Home! I will follow Mother Nature home away from foolish mortals
Who believes they will never die.
They will die and so will I, but before that time comes
I will teach them to see past the branches of the forest.
All the way up to the clear sky.
With the stars shining brightly in their set positions.
They are the souls who have gone before me.
Those who have realized that the ancestors were wrong.
Like fools in the darkness you make your way through
The forest of shadows.
Ghastly-deformed trees and vines grab at you
From above and behind,

But if you give me your hand I will show you the way out.
To a clear lake where you can cleanse your mind of ignorance,
And wash your skin with the knowledge of how to
Save this frail and crippling existence
Which we call humanity.

"the mistakes of our parents in the 50's-70's...
politically, environmentally, physically (e.g. drugs)"

Sara Cook
Spencer, IA, USA

The Living

thrashing, the soul pounds the dirt
lying in agony and wishing away a life not lived
defeat holds strongly, as hope runs away
and still the echo calls back evermore

i cannot understand such sorrow
for i have never seen that place,
though this soul is knowing of loneliness' deep chasm

and what can i offer?
these dead tokens which time has called the truth?
remnants of lost peace and strength?
no, i cannot hold out this,
nor can i give a soul its strength

to be alive is not to hide among the fallacies of thinkers,
those, who in their quest to impart such truths
gave but a sword of pain

life is not a cell
in which to live on borrowed fantasies,
not a hollowed shell of ages gone

we who are here--we are the living
those souls which pass from time to time
giving as they move,
taking not what days have given

i cannot understand the pain
so many live within,
i cannot know the wounds which still remain unhealed,
but give these words as they've been formed
and simply say, "i live."

Vanessa M. Brown
Lakeland, FL, USA

View from a Padded Room

To be sane
in an insane world
has to be one
of the most
craziest ideas
ever dreamt up
by somebody
sitting in the corner
of a rubber circle room
with a painted view
of the outside,
drawn by someone
secluded from the sunlight
except for the light bulb
flickering in and out
of brightness like a faded
Christmas bulb on a tree.
It's all like a rusted Ferris wheel
where you hope for
one more trip round
and if you do
you're gracious for the sparks
but despise the bolts
that hold it all together.
Laugh when laughter
is hollow
and meaningless
for then and only then
may you find true humour.
Cry when you're strong and
hold an ace up your sleeve,
be prepared for tomorrow
when there's no
tomorrow in sight.
To be insane
in a sane world
is only a fantasy
for sanity,
in reality,
is someone's warped
view
of mental brutality.

*"In life there are masks and
illusions…search and your
heart will let you see the
truth"*

Terry Dean Reimer
Peachland, BC, Canada

Changeling

*She left me
designer clothes
yellowed books
and bad poetry.
The dead child is
in closets and drawers
scents and sights
slice of sky and
mountains. I see
through her eyes but
can't look into them.
She was gut acid
and blood tears
rolling into a pink
satin box, her sharp
edges covered with
lace and plastic
pearls. She lived
through dried ink on
pages, feeding off
people who never
existed, eating their
strength, devouring
their wickedness,
lapping their grief
until she was erased
by too much want -
to become, to imitate
to become identical
to become a sham.
I took her place
from too much want -
to be, to stand
to be original
to be real.
Now she's a ghost
girl screaming death
threats in my head
on snowy nights
a reality away
so I look for chinks
in her dainty shell
but all I find is
innocence dumped
in malice, shredded
into permanent doubt,
the same one caged
in my ribs. And she
laughs, she laughs,
she laughs.*

*"a renewed woman who cannot get
rid of the person she wishes to
annihilate - herself"*

Annepely P. Dakay-Liquigan
Irving, TX, USA

bLiND DEAF AND DEAD

Too mUcH NoIse.
Too mUch liGht.
All thEsE colOrs
Are maKIng Me BLIND
AlL theSe voices;
aRe makInG me DEAF.

TheSe finGErs aroUND my Neck.
They're taking   my   air.
They're   draw ing my   blood.

CoLoUrS and NoiSE.
One whirlwind of life.
One whirlwind of ???

Gordon Calleja
Floriana, Malta

Not Far

The flowers have bloomed,
And trees rustling.
The breeze is caressing,
And sun warm.
You are somewhere very close.
There is a feeling of freedom,
An experience of boldness.
There is a burst of jubilance,
An air of confidence.
You are somewhere very close.
I can sense your presence,
But not touch, hear or feel.
I am drawn towards you,
As if by an ecstatic trance.
You are somewhere very close.

"written under an attack of nostalgia…
memories of happy times flew by as if they were real"

Aaju / Bharadwaj Raghuraman
Karnataka, India

Late Nights

Alone, alone
I sit, alone
To madness prone,
I sit
Alone.

I sit, and sit
And yearn to spit
Or laugh or cry
Or simply die
Or learn to fly
I can but try
Since my spirit lies
Alone.

No new e-mail,
No chats prevail
No flashing lights
This lonely night
No soulful songs
Will come along
To keep me
Company.

They've all gone out
And if I shout
There is no one near
Enough to hear
This pathetic plea
This isn't me!
My smile is faded,
I am simply jaded
At this wasted night
With no strength to fight
The fact
That I sit,
Alone.

*"scribbled hastily late one Friday night
whilst I slaved over homework assignments
and realized I was the only one in the universe sitting at home"*

Gila Monster
Montreal, Quebec, Canada

Withdrawal

hot unbearable
sweat against
sobbing cotton:

a body begs
arms curl
hands reach
each to find only itself

and shakes
a pillow aches
with only one
head against it.

in the imprint
the fading hollow
your body carved
dull shadows lurk
lack substance
cannot be held.

in the quivering night
your whispered quick
insisting breath
lingers in the air
escapes the ear
is almost heard
as it vanishes.

in the pulse
the shuddering soft
primal rush
a cadence is diminished
a percussion left
only to itself,
lonely, a wandering loss...

in emptiness
in voids unfilled
here you are held
roaring in silence
raw, impassioned impulses
striving against conviction.

night yawns on,
swallows all.

B. D. Gaines
Los Angeles, CA, USA

that which used to heal me
starts to hurt
and everything that could harm
just turns me cold
as an enough seen picture
a song looped to angst
my spirit feels pain
it's just inertia
days will come slow and endless
and empty
as always
but it doesn't matter anymore
everyone's got a cross
and mine is too small
sometimes
when fear holds my smile
and my steps are guided by this lack
i wonder how life would be
if i really could believe
for instance in you
but we both know
it's impossible

"even pain has its advantages...
there's nothing worse than going
cold, while life bleeds you...the lack
of pain - an abstinence syndrome"

Alvaro r. Lopez
Antofagasta, Chile

I'm a philosopher.
I'm a dead woman
in a grave that'll never be.
Take a breath of life.
I didn't give you away
and I can never bring you back.
I can only let you be.

Jennie Walker
Auburn, AL, USA

You Think Lies

Who that opens part way is wrong
Who curls the shyness in black
And you think
You illuminate my thoughts
But can't you see
Everyone's wants are unbearable
There are no wanted pains for mother and father
And you think
Who could have bruised my arms
But can't you see
That it was me
And there is white fire dancing
With the reflection I am not
And you think
You own smiles crying of my person
Quiet, no shouts for me
Can't you just see it
And time is chipping my lies
The wrong done dirty water
And you think
All headaches are lost from tears
But enemies are untying my shoes
Can't you see
And knowing the one and going exactly
The floor is on the wall
Did you know that
And the boys bended my late fingers
As you excitedly watched
And you think
It's all associated with drumming hyenas
But I know who scribbled my stars
Can't you see that
And there are older peaches of this aroma
Real blended originalities
Did you see that
The constant thumping
Never repeating anger
One tangled day
And you think
I'm the opposite of real rigid nails
But there's a lake melting psychoticness
Did you know that
And the invisible ceiling is widening
I know that

Rachel Favinger, age 17
Bethlehem, PA, USA

Budding Glory

I can taste your breath
But you don't lie upon my chest
I can't see you
But I know you smell good

I look at you through glass
Though you're perfect

I can scratch the glass...and laugh
Because I know you're smiling

Your songs are sung by the trees-
Like the trees leaves are changing color
You are changing in my mind

Later, I'll see the trees
When they are green again
I'll smell your flowers too
They'll both sing to me
Tauntingly...hopefully, its budding glory

Your beautiful music of love
And desire to want what I want...

and need.

Katie
Paynesville, MN, USA

There In Your Eyes   (for John Lewis...)

It's there in your eyes,
    Narrowed against the blinding sunlight,
I see the agony of your helplessness,
    Unable to face the pain
        Inside...

I know the demons that haunt you,
    In your restless sleep,
And are always whispering to you,
    Unceasingly while you're
        Awake...

Forever are you troubled,
    Your senses constantly assailed,
Held hostage by the evil ravages,
    Of an unrelenting
        Despair...

And I, knowing what you are,
    And fearing what you will become,
Shared in your helplessness.
    If only you could have shared it
        With me...

"to all who are troubled at heart. May you find peace in the comfort of your loved ones"

Gregory B. Banks
Stockbridge, GA, USA

SUBWAY

anything to steal the mind away-
desperate ocean shore.
and the narcotic balm sleeping like...
dew, on the desert floor.
Excuse me miss, with your lips pursed-
wondering if I gave you the impression;
no, better still,
if you somehow guessed (by my eyes or...)
oh,
seems you have to leave.
Well,
only good things go away.
and here it sits
promising to stay forever!
ah, but by this time all is forever.
the pulsing at my temples, the shaking of these hands,
the embers behind these eyes.
And in the pit- the very basest bottom even!
grows a hunger for
(no, not love even- not this night)
only understanding.

Anything to steal the mind away-
the elderly shaking returns to youthful hands;
but what really is age?
(but a curse)
When I sit back, glancing up-
the florescent lights still sting
and I recall the thoughts:
the metal staircase,
moving endlessly without a soul to climb her!
In complete solitude,
with no one watching nor noticing.
But,
come stranger to beg my hand
come stranger to fly me off into the night.
My time has so endlessly come;
and so I dissolve-
still rejecting that which resembles me,
that which reflects me.
The lights scream past my head,
and the night
(overwhelmed by plastic day)
takes my material self over land and sea.
Looking for ANYTHING,
to steal the mind away.

*"lack of imagination and attention span...emotion and thought being
eradicated under the influence of flashing TV images and a pop-culture
state of flux"*

Jereme Micheal Riley, age 19
Edmonton, AB, Canada

Independence

If I asked you about Poetry
you'd read me a nice rhyme.
Tell me about the masters
Their lives their work, their time.

    If I asked you about love
    You'd answer me with theory
    about how love does not exist
    and life is dark and dreary.

If I asked you about war
you'd tell me every date
of every major conflict
in every nationstate.

    If I asked you about anything
    You'd tell me with a look
    every single thought you have
    or read from a text book.

But you've never written a meaningful word
and never been in love.
You've never been near any war
to know what I speak of.

    So free me from your ignorance.
    Emancipate my ears.
    I claim my independence
    'til your living's matched your years.

Wm. Gregg Bridgeman
Smithfield, NC, USA

EVERYWHERE

WOULD HAVE FOLLOWED THEM
A THOUSAND TIMES AGAIN
THEIR MINDS, THEIR MEMORY

ALWAYS SEARCHING
FOR WHAT HAPPENED
IS NOT MINE

KNOWING:
NEVER WILL IT BE ALIKE

*"searching for someone else's memories,
striving to gain them, coming to realize that they're not for us to see"*

Torsten C. Kathke
Ulm, Germany

fucking nonsensical trials

yes,
i am not hiding the fact
that i have been down alleyways of
too much use truth be told.
my cluttered heart plunged into loving
and blurred the distinction
between straightforwardness
and zipping buttons undone.
and hell yes
i'm declining to reenter doorways unaccustomed to my
overzealousness...
and sit before a family
of inferior to none-but-god,
and stand while standards
not my own are judging
me not right.
and fuck yes
i refuse, with abhorrence, to unfold my hands and slash wrists in
hoped
forgiveness
but not forgiven..
and be driven
with repentance faked for scrutiny of
those feathered fluffs of non-emotion
emotionally boggled by my current passivity.
oh yea,
and with them looking on a
cruel,
blatantly naked smile grows
just because i want it to.

jessica garver
Madison, WI, USA

African Children   *(for my mother)*

Among the trees the stunted girl
Turned back, into the hidden world.
The ragged boy ran on ahead,
Home to the kingdom of the dead.

But I will never let them go,
Come the concrete, come the snow,
Come the colors in the night,
My high window in the light.
I will go along behind,
Mute and lame and deaf and blind.

There is no effect or cause
To guess, no statutory clause
To cite, no tourist magazine
To tell what mystery I have seen.

But I will never let them be,
Come the highway, come the sea,
The radio, the dunes around,
The open window's glare of sound.
I trail the children to the birth
Of none of us in all the earth.

"memories from a Sunday morning walk in Lesotho"

Sarah Ruden
Baltimore, MD, USA

A Question Of Numbers

fingers in the throat
like a gunshot awakening
i have no strings left to cut
please help me to hear your words
for i have spoken an ignorance for far too long
undying habits
knifed in the face
i have no walls left to bury
so there was you
such is life
so they say
slide your blood soaked hands behind my ears
i will help you up
so i may knock you down again
a relapse in my integrity
cleaned
i've had my nose in this plastic flower for long enough
but i refuse to burn all bridges
i have unnecessarily crossed
for that is much too wasteful
raised arms in passion
but not in prayer this time
this is not a comfort
believe me
but i must not play "pin the tail on the savior" anymore
i must move on
there has to be something
but you're not it

Commovere
Derry, NH, USA

LOOK MA! I'M A DEMOGRAPHIC!

My gay pride credit card
Has a higher interest rate
Than the generic Visa I could get at my bank
The gay resorts are pricey
And the guys in the ads are too buff
Much more buff than I am
My gay long-distance company
Donates ten percent
When I spend ten percent more per minute
And if I buy a polo shirt
With a gay symbol stitched on the pocket
I'll pay forty or fifty bucks
I can't afford to be proud.

"after being shunned as a minority by mainstream society, now the advertising man is trying to make a buck using my newfound freedom"

Coke Brown, Jr.
Venus, TX, USA

Memories and Reality Time

Tears emersing in long distance from help on the battlefield of life so entangling with trees and forests and green pea soup of murky water and cleanful dirt just folded pages with love entwined saying hello speaking with heart beating picture painting a photograph of holding onto mindscapes of a broken portrait all alone with signatures and autographs of friends holding hands and singing songs of words and phrases pen and ink the prom queens and the suicide teens but still the games and games and fun fun fun and jokes and poor excuses just careless memories wandering in madness of the architecture texture turning green and purple black and orange red and blue and brown the quick of the auto fuzzing light stream racing then the change to campus hopping of extreme insomniac raids of plastic food and plastic cups of cellophane the sunglasses night and vampirisitic spiritual mornings of drinking liquid sugar and crystalline caffeine just to laugh and joke and scream and cry and then just broken down and then just fixed and working the slumbersome suntime the dreary always feeling just gothic dressing black and blasting amperage crowdstanding dancesharing and then saying hi to denny and saying bye eventually to memorizing of memories and the stance trance dance must soon click back to what but reality time.

"how nostalgia helps us face our boring lives, while staying realistic and dumping mysticism"

T. S. Hunter
Glendora, CA, USA

Some Comfort Here

This glorious sadness
Touches all it meets
To bring down to tears
      To knees.
The sorrow that rises,
From places dreamt
Within you.

The light of your
Eyes lay upon
The river as your
Sauntering stares land there.

Tiny ripples from
Your core make
The heart grow and open
Like tears in a wound.

The howling of
Your only friends
Makes hands quiver
And bend, slightly;
As if to some unsounded note
That awakens us to ourselves.

The masks dissolve into
The salty wastes of our eyes
And we weep , vulnerable
      like birds fallen from their nests.
All I think now : I want to be back home :
Home : The place I remember in my complacent sorrows.

Ivo Visic
Johannesburg, South Africa

Speak Your Mind

You look at me and see I am different.
You watch every move I make
And hear everything I say
As your mind takes a picture of me
Which will be used against me in the future.
The stereotypes you hear day in and day out
Tell you that I'm different,
Therefore I don't care about anything
And I don't have any feelings,
So you continue to mock me
And criticize me every opportunity you get.
For some reason,
You're too stupid
To understand that you're different from me, too,
And that I could apply the same stereotypes to you.
I'm not afraid of what's different,
And I'm not afraid to speak my mind,
So I'm telling you now
That contrary to popular belief,
I *do* have feelings,
And I *do* care.
Possibly not for the same reasons and about the same things,
But I'd like to think that you are human
And also have feelings.
So I've had my turn,
Now it's time to speak *your* mind.

Elizabeth Brown
Bloomsdale, MO, USA

an x'ers free form view of what?

generation x?
sounds funky and cool,
like a madison avenue-packaged soft drink
or some new basketball shoe.
but it's a stupid label,
a convenient tag invented by some advertising maven
who couldn't find anything else to pin on us.
but what the hell does it mean?
is it supposed to unite us?
define us?
set us apart from those who went before
or from those who come after?
not fucking likely.
what the hell is "x" anyway?

stuck in the middle between
the boomers and now,
we're more an accident of birth
than a movement of history.
we're not a cultural movement,
we're not a wellspring of political thought.
but hell, we're IT apparently -
the marketers want our cash,
decision makers want our votes.
we're the torch bearers
for our page in history
but we don't give a shit -
none of us wants the poisoned chalice
that our confused, self-absorbed forebears
are going to pass onto us.
they were going to change the world,
they just kept the treadmill going
and expect us to run it for them
when it's time for them to move on.
but its confusing being in a nether world
that actually doesn't exist
no distinctions, no philosophies.
what's our music?
what's our art?
what were our defining moments?
walls coming down? aids?
the new world order (fries or a drink with your order?

what drove us other than those before,
obsessed with the idea
that we should have what they had
and want what they wanted
as empty and pointless as it may have been.
growing up an x-er
in a battleground between the boomers
and those before them,
stuck slap bang in the middle
with the happy hippies on one side
and morose fatalism on the other.

"a label created by some faceless, nameless people in suits, `X' borders on the insulting...sometimes treated with derision by the generation before, their revolutionary zeal come to naught...are they taking it out on us?"

Mike Augustin
Perth, Western Australia

"mwe" is considering bringing out a "**volume 2**" of *In Our Own Words*.   Submission will be accepted from **May through October 1999**.   If your birth date is within the range of the years **1961** to **1982**, send your poetry to

mwe@interpath.com

or

MWE
3903 Captial Blvd., Suite 194
Raleigh, NC 27604, USA

"mwe" is also considering a poetry anthology under the working title "**Booming Silence**", and seeking poetry that addresses the cultural/social transition of the so-called "boomers" from the 1960's through the 1990's. Your birth year should fall into the range of the years **1945 to 1960**. Submissions will be accepted **up to the end of 1999**.